Touring

CALIFORNIA AND NEVADA HOT SPRINGS

Matt C. Bischoff

FALCON®

GUILFORD, CONNECTICUT
HELENA, MONTANA

AN IMPRINT OF THE GLOBE PEQUOT PRESS

A FALCON GUIDE®

Copyright ©1997 by The Globe Pequot Press
Previously published by Falcon Publishing, Inc.

Cover photo by Mark E. Gibson.
All black-and-white photos by the author.

Library of Congress Cataloging-in-Publication Data
    Bischoff, Matt C.
        Touring California & Nevada hot springs / Matt C. Bischoff.
            p.   cm.
        ISBN 1-56044-578-5 (pbk.)
            1. Hot springs—California—Guidebooks.   2. Hot springs—Nevada—Guidebooks.   I. Title.
        GB1198.3.C2B57 1997
        613'.122'025794—dc21   97-14037
                                                                         CIP

Manufactured in the United States of America
First Edition/Fifth Printing

CAUTION

Outdoor recreational activities are by their very nature potentially hazardous. All participants in such activities must assume the responsibility for their own actions and safety. The information contained in this guidebook cannot replace sound judgment and good decision-making skills, which help reduce risk exposure, nor does the scope of this book allow for disclosure of all the potential hazards and risks involved in such activities.

Learn as much as possible about the outdoor recreational activities in which you participate, prepare for the unexpected, and be cautious. The reward will be a safer and more enjoyable experience.

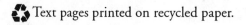 Text pages printed on recycled paper.

To Dr. James L. Bischoff,
who first introduced me to hot springs
and shared his enthusiasm for these geological wonders.

CONTENTS

SOUTHERN NEVADA

NORTHERN CALIFORNIA

SOUTHERN CALIFORNIA

OVERVIEW MAP

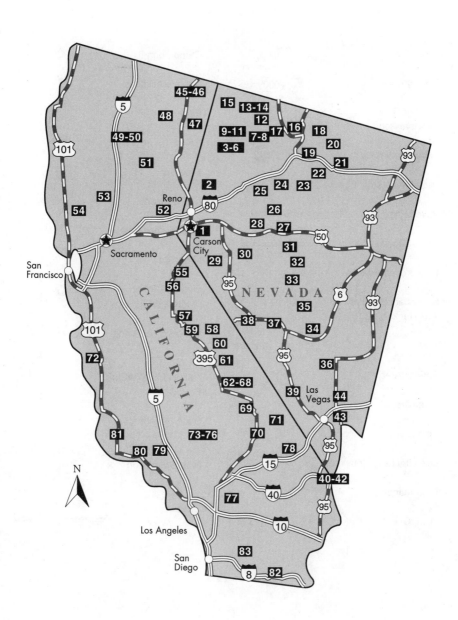

MAP LEGEND

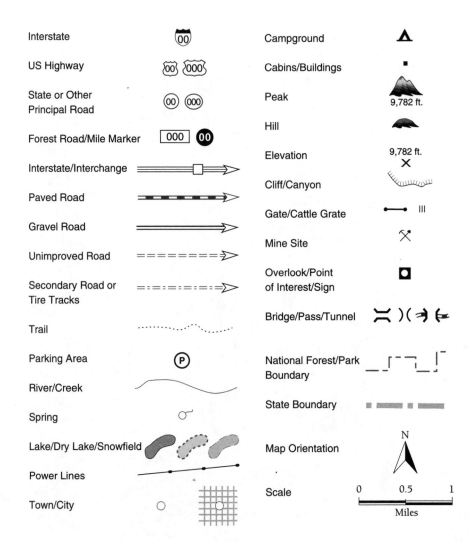

Interstate		Campground	
US Highway		Cabins/Buildings	
State or Other Principal Road		Peak	9,782 ft.
Forest Road/Mile Marker	000 00	Hill	
Interstate/Interchange		Elevation	9,782 ft.
Paved Road		Cliff/Canyon	
Gravel Road		Gate/Cattle Grate	III
Unimproved Road		Mine Site	
Secondary Road or Tire Tracks		Overlook/Point of Interest/Sign	
Trail		Bridge/Pass/Tunnel	
Parking Area	P	National Forest/Park Boundary	
River/Creek		State Boundary	
Spring			
Lake/Dry Lake/Snowfield		Map Orientation	N
Power Lines			
Town/City		Scale	0 0.5 1 Miles

Vichy Springs' Olympic size pool with Vichy Creek and forest behind.

INTRODUCTION

HOT SPRINGS IN HISTORY

Hissing steam vents, erupting geysers, boiling mud pots, and bubbling springs of hot water issuing naturally from the earth are fascinating and mysterious things to behold. Long before recorded history, ancient people used hot springs for bathing and food preparation. According to archaeological evidence, balneology—the utilization of natural mineral waters for the treatment of disease—has been practiced for more than five thousand years.

Hot springs have been used in religious rites and ceremonies in both Egypt and the Middle East for centuries. The ancient Greeks and Romans were addicted to the pleasures of spas and built important communities around natural hot springs, harnessing and channeling thermal waters into elaborate buildings and colossal public baths. The Japanese have particularly enjoyed such a tradition from their ancient past to the present, and a visit to a traditional Japanese hot spring resort today is a special pleasure. The Victorian era in Europe saw a rebirth of interest in spas, particularly for medicinal benefits attributed to drinking the waters, although bathing was still an important activity. A visit to a spa became a fashionable pastime for wealthy Europeans, and thermal waters that earlier had been exploited by Romans were developed into elaborate resort-hotel complexes.

On this continent, Native Americans have used hot springs as campsites, village locations, and sacred places for untold years. As illustrated in this book, evidence of native use of hot springs remains today. Soon after Europeans arrived in North America, they discovered and exploited hot springs. As people sought a more civilized way of bathing, resorts and spas became the answer, allowing for private and controlled use of the medicinal waters. The popularity with which hot spring resorts were received in Europe eventually spilled over into America, and such places were particularly popular from the 1880s through the turn of the last century. Resorts were built at locations such as Hot Springs, Arkansas; Saratoga Springs, New York; Warm Springs, Georgia; and White Sulphur Springs, West Virginia. Because of limited population and lack of governmental support, however, these springs never became as elaborate as their European counterparts.

Hot springs began to be harnessed for use in resorts during the Victorian period and flourished just before the dawn of the twentieth century. Remains of such development at countless hot springs in the West attest to this boom time in commercial hot spring bathing. Resorts generally promised that their hot spring waters had preventative and curative values. By the turn of the century, transportation had vastly improved, allowing people to reach places in days, that would have taken weeks otherwise. The arrival of the automobile also increased the mobility of Americans, allowing many people to visit resorts across the country.

The fashion waned by the outbreak of the First World War, but by that time all the major thermal areas of the East had been developed. In the West, development of thermal waters was much less extensive because of a much smaller population density. By the 1950s, the boom in hot spring resorts had passed. Many commercial springs closed down or were simply abandoned; many of these have never been reopened. Today, an increased interest in hot springs has resulted in the reuse of previously abandoned springs, with varying results.

Despite their decline in popularity, hot springs continue to be used for a variety of purposes. In many places in the world, particularly in Europe and Japan, hot springs are still used for medical purposes. Hot springs are believed by millions to aid prevention and treatment of a variety of ailments. Today there are an estimated 1,800 hot springs in the United States, the majority of which are in the West. Of those hot springs, slightly more than a hundred have been developed into extensive resorts or spas.

GEOLOGY OF HOT SPRINGS

Peering into warm mineral springs, one gets the distinct feeling that one is viewing the interior of the earth. That is not far from the truth.

Much is known about the geological setting of hot springs, which are the surface manifestation of what geologists term geothermal systems. Many of these systems have been tapped for the generation of electricity, since they act as a clean source of energy to replace fossil fuels. Hot springs on the surface of the earth can be no hotter than the boiling point at the earth's surface (212 degrees Fahrenheit, or 100 degrees Celsius). Waters at depth, however, can reach temperatures as high as 752 degrees F. (400 degrees C.)! Such super temperatures are possible because the boiling point is raised by high hydrostatic pressure at great depth, and because of the water's nearness to subsurface molten rock.

The earth's heat originates deep beneath its crust through the decaying of natural radioactive elements such as uranium, thorium, and potassium. Hot springs generally occur where hot or molten rock exists at relatively shallow depths. Areas of recent or active volcanic activity (for instance, Lassen Volcanic National Park) are obvious examples of such locales.

Although hot springs are abundant in these regions, the most prevalent and spectacular ones are on the sea floor, far from human view. These underwater springs occur along chains of active submarine volcanoes called spreading centers, places where the earth's plates diverge. Hot springs can also occur in

Geology of Hot Springs

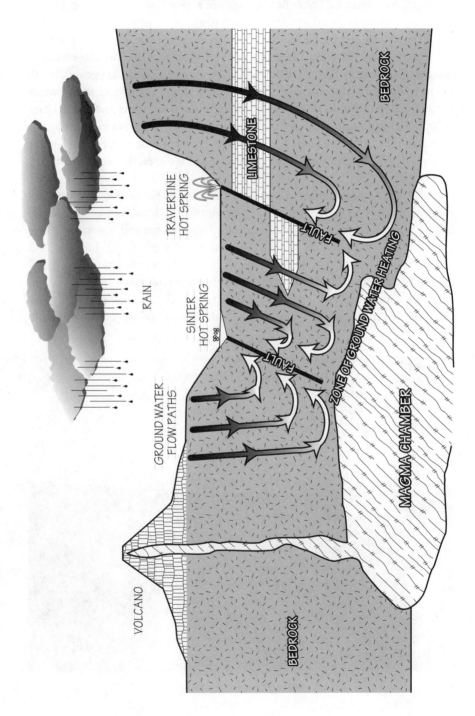

places where there is no obvious source for heating the water—far from volcanic areas, for example. These hot springs are formed where there are magma bodies, at depth, with no surface manifestation, or where the water itself has come from great depths, forced to the surface by some unexplained means.

Hot springs occur because of convection. Water acts like air above a radiator, rising and expanding as it's heated. Since the earth's rocks are generally full of cracks and fractures, these inevitably become filled with water as rainwater percolates downward to fill the voids. Collected in the porous rocks, this water is kept as ground water. In mountainous regions, it sometimes emerges again, forced to the surface by some impermeable barrier. These natural, cold-water springs, downhill from the water's entry point into the earth, occur because of simple gravity flow.

The convective process, not gravity, gives rise to hot springs. Ground water near recently injected molten rock becomes very hot, even boiling. Such heated water is less dense than the surrounding cold ground water, so it rises toward the surface. As it does, cold water instantaneously moves into the void around the magma to replace the rising water. The system functions like a coffee percolator. The heated water rises and mixes with overlying water as it rises, and loses some of its heat to the rocks through which it passes, eventually discharging at the surface as a hot spring. The pathway of ascent is commonly

Jackson Mountain Hot Spring.

along a fault because of ease of flow (see diagram). Once such convection systems are set up they can last for hundreds of years as heat is slowly harvested from the magma, forcing it to cool and solidify. Water flow, temperatures, and the chemical composition of such hot spring waters often remain stable for long periods of time in spite of year-to-year variation in rainfall, suggesting that a spring's complex plumbing systems can be very deep and large.

The chemical composition of thermal waters is controlled by the rocks through which they pass. Some hot springs deposit calcium carbonate-rich travertine around their orifices—Travertine Hot Spring (described in this book), or Mammoth Hot Springs in Yellowstone National Park, for example. Water from these springs leaches and dissolves calcium carbonate from limestone under the earth's surface. When the thermal waters discharge at ground level, the water effervesces dissolved carbon dioxide gas in the same way soda pop effervesces when the bottle cap is removed. This releases the calcium carbonate from the water, and deposits it at the spring mouth.

In most volcanically active regions where limestone is not present, hot springs deposit siliceous sinter around their orifices. Sinter is relatively pure silica, has the same composition as quartz, and is the most common constituent of igneous rocks. At room temperature, silica is almost insoluble—we use it in making glass. At high temperatures, deep in geothermal systems, however, silica is relatively soluble, so thermal waters leach silica from the rocks. As the water discharges, it becomes supersaturated with silica which precipitates as sinter when the spring cools. These two types of chemical deposits, sinter and travertine, are quite different in character, and tell us much about the subsurface geology through which the hot waters passed.

HOW TO USE THIS BOOK

BOOK ORGANIZATION

California and Nevada are the largest producers of geothermal power in the country. In fact, California produces more geothermal energy than anywhere else in the world. Despite the abundance of harnessed hot springs in these two states, there are plenty that are still in their natural form.

This guide to hot springs does not pretend to be an exhaustive list of hot springs and resorts in California and Nevada. Instead it is a guide to some of the best hot springs in the West. Most springs in this book are natural springs in natural settings. Of the many hot spring resorts in California and Nevada, I included only those that are particularly enjoyable, have natural pools on their property, or are in a picturesque or historic setting. This book also is not strictly a guide to hot spring soaking, though most of the springs described offer wonderful bathing experiences. Included are several worth visiting simply for interest's sake. Before you visit any of these springs, please read the precautions and etiquette tips below.

The book is organized geographically to allow for the greatest ease in traveling from one hot spring to the next. Following a short introduction to the spring, all pertinent information you will need for a visit is provided. Each entry lists subjects such as location, access, time of year, and nearest services. The detailed set of directions given for each spring is followed by a more in-depth discussion and description of the spring itself.

The book is divided into six parts: Northern California, Central California, Southern California, Northern Nevada, Central Nevada, and Southern Nevada. Each hot spring is placed within one of these regions. In some cases, a hot spring in one region may be closer to springs in another region than to those in its own. For example, Saratoga Hot Spring (in Central Nevada) is closer to Steamboat Hot Springs (in Northern Nevada) than it is to any other spring in its region. Regional lines were drawn arbitrarily for the sake of organization. To find nearby springs in surrounding regions, check the **Overview Map**.

The book is also divided into subregions. These subregions also were created arbitrarily, although they are designed to give the reader a sense of place when visiting a hot spring or series of hot springs. These subregions follow geographical, archaeological, or historical lines. A short introduction points out some of the more salient features of the surrounding country. In several places historical vignettes add flavor to the regional description, putting the reader far ahead of the casual tourist, who generally knows nothing about the area's past.

How to Follow Directions and Maps

Each set of directions in this book is designed to be used in conjunction with the maps provided. These directions have all been field checked and should get you to the spring with minimal confusion. The maps provided show important features needed for reaching the spring, but readers need to pay close attention to mileages stated in the **"Finding the spring"** portion of the entry. Maps do not always show all the features in the region, and ours are designed to be locational aids, not replacements for a topographic map.

For best results, use a standard highway map and a USGS topographic map when visiting these springs. The topographic map quadrangle name is listed under "Maps" in each spring description. These maps can be ordered directly from the USGS for $5 each (plus postage). They can also be found at many map stores, and some specialty outdoors outlets. In several cases, as noted, you may wish to obtain a Forest Service map for the region; the phone number for each forest's managing agency is listed. Important information—such as up-to-date road conditions, access, permit requirements, and weather data—can usually be found in the offices of area land management agencies. Contact them before you go.

Precautions

Visiting hot springs carries with it certain risks and inherent dangers. Hot springs, after all, can contain scalding water. Pay attention to all directions and descriptions given in this book, and realize that not all dangers can be anticipated. Do not, under any circumstance, get into water without first testing it in some way. You will usually be able to tell how hot a spring is just by coming near the water. If you can feel heat from a few inches away, or if the water is steaming, even on a warm day, it is probably too hot. If the water appears to be fine, put a finger or hand in the water first to test it. If your hand can't stay submerged without hurting, don't put your body in. More importantly, if you cannot see the bottom of a spring, don't get in. Water on the top of the spring may be fine, but deeper water may scald you. Also be careful around mud in hot springs, since it often hides extremely hot water underneath. When in doubt, stay out.

Many springs are far from civilization, so take appropriate precautions. Be sure your vehicle is in sound shape and able to make a long trip. Check the engine's fluids, including oil and coolant. Be sure that your tires have the necessary pressure, and that you have a spare (along with a jack and lug wrench). Know how to change a tire before you head out. The most common breakdown, by far, is a flat tire, and driving on dirt roads you will eventually get one. Rocks have a tendency to get caught in your treads, occasionally puncturing the fabric of the tire. Also plan ahead when considering gasoline. Be sure you know how far you are going, what your gas mileage is, and where the next place is that you can purchase gasoline. Nearby services are listed in each of this book's entries.

If you plan on camping, make a checklist of equipment needed before heading out. Bring at least the following:

- spare tire, jack, lug wrench
- basic tool kit for the car (screwdrivers, wrenches, hammer, etc.)
- shelter of some kind (tent, tarp, etc.)
- extra clothing (including wet weather gear)
- sleeping bag, insulating pad, and blankets
- food and water (more than you will need)
- stove or other means by which to cook food
- electrical tape
- rope
- shovel
- ax or small saw
- firewood
- candles
- matches
- flashlights
- extra batteries
- knife
- first-aid kit

Once you have packed all this gear, be sure to notify someone of your trip, and when you plan on returning. Even if you plan to be out for the day only, it's not a bad idea to bring along most of this equipment—you'll be glad you did if you get stranded. Contact the land managing agency for the area into which you are heading and ask about access, restrictions, and permit requirements. Be sure to watch the weather. If storms threaten, stay off secondary dirt roads even if you have four-wheel drive; keep off all dirt roads if you have a passenger vehicle. A road may be dry when you depart but can become impassable during and following a storm. In desert portions of California and Nevada, be especially aware of thunderstorms and flash floods. Flash floods can occur even when it is not raining where you are. Desert washes can fill with no warning and become raging torrents. Do not under any circumstances make camp in a wash.

RESPONSIBLE BEHAVIOR

Visiting hot springs carries with it an unspoken etiquette. Since most of the hot springs described in this book are on public land, you will not be trespassing when you visit them. But a few springs are located on private land, in which case we recommend you do not trespass. In some cases, the landowner has allowed people to visit the springs on his or her property. In any case, respect private property, and ask before you go. If there are "no trespassing" signs, obey them. This will prevent you from getting shot, and will help to keep numerous hot springs open to the public. Also obey all public land signs. In several cases, overnight camping is not permitted, and such rules are usually posted. There are usually campgrounds or other public lands that do not restrict camping nearby.

One of the biggest problems faced by hot spring enthusiasts is vandalism and trash. Most well-known hot springs have experienced some aspect of these. Graffiti, broken glass, litter, and off-road driving truly detract from the beauty of these places. Be sure to pack out all trash, stay on established roads, and generally leave things as you found them—or better.

Many of the hot springs described in this book are quite popular. Do not be surprised when you find people already at your hot spring destination. People generally prefer privacy, and will appreciate it if you let them finish their soak before you enjoy the water. This is especially true for families and couples. Others may enjoy your company, and a simple inquiry will let you know either way. Many locations offer several soaking opportunities, sometimes quite removed from the other pools.

A word about nudity: many people enjoy hot springs in a natural state. For hot springs in remote locations, this is the norm. Most public bathing facilities or pools in public view generally require bathing suits, unless you have a private room. You will see the prevalent trend at most springs. Obey any and all signs posted and you should have no problem. In several localities, nudity has become pervasive—visitors to these springs prefer to go without clothes for just about every activity. Some locations where nudity is prevalent include Deep Creek Hot Springs, Saline Valley Hot Springs, and the Long Valley Hot Springs. Some of the resorts in this book allow visitors to remain nude in the pool areas—among these are Sierra and Tecopa hot springs. If nudity offends you, you may not want to visit these places. Or you may wish to wait until you can have the locality to yourself.

AUTHOR'S FAVORITES

For an Isolated Experience

Black Rock Hot Spring. On the margins of an immense dry lake, only accessible during a few months, Black Rock Hot Spring truly gives you a feeling of isolation. The large, black rock formation from which the hot spring derives its name has long been a beacon for travelers. Native Americans used the spring as a campsite. For emigrants headed to Oregon and California in the mid-nineteenth century, the black rock and its spring served as a milestone and camp. Today, the spring has changed little. A historical marker, placed by an overland trails club, reminds visitors of the historical significance of the spot. A Bureau of Land Management sign reminds one of the twentieth century.

The hot spring can only be reached by traveling across the Black Rock Desert Playa, a worthy experience in itself. For only a short three months the playa is safe to cross—otherwise the mud becomes wet and undriveable. Occasionally, the mighty prehistoric lake bed becomes an actual lake again, giving one a glimpse back to the Pleistocene Epoch when large mammals roamed the same country. Remains of a mammoth was discovered on this very playa, dating back more than ten thousand years.

Hot Spring Near the City

Big Caliente and Little Caliente Hot Springs. The two Caliente Hot Springs lie in the rugged mountains above Santa Barbara. Although the road to the springs is long, windy, and dirt surfaced for much of its distance, the springs can easily be visited in a day from Santa Barbara. The best seasons in which to visit are fall and spring, since summers can be too hot to make bathing enjoyable and winter rains may make the road impassable.

Located within Los Padres National Forest, Big and Little Caliente Hot Springs see a high volume of visitors throughout the year, particularly on weekends. There are numerous campgrounds, picnic areas, and countless trails for hiking and mountain biking. Your best chance for seclusion comes midweek.

Most Amazing Geologic Feature

Diana's Punch Bowl. This hot spring is the most visually spectacular in the book, and the most amazing one I've ever seen. A huge travertine hill marks its location from miles away. In the middle of this huge hill is a gigantic cavern, extending into the hill about 30 feet. At the bottom, crystal-clear hot spring water forms a large pool. You can then see another 10 or 20 feet into the spring itself, a window to the interior of the earth.

In addition to the spectacular nature of this spring, there are bathing opportunities (but don't even think of trying to get into the cavern). Along the flank of the hill several small pools of varying temperature offer a view of the beautiful Monitor Valley. This hot spring is near several other interesting sites, most notably the ghost town of Belmont to the west.

Most Popular Spring with Everyone Else

Travertine Hot Spring. Close to the highway and easy to reach, Travertine Hot Spring has seen a rapid increase in visitors the past five years. No wonder. The spring is another fascinating geologic feature, exhibiting a prominent ridge of travertine. The scenery is unparalleled, with a view of the Bridgeport Valley and the mighty Sierras beyond. Bathing opportunities are fantastic. The upper pool has been meticulously maintained by dedicated volunteers, and the lower ones offer a more natural bathing experience. The water temperature is also ideal. U.S. Highway 395 is a well-traveled highway, carrying skiers headed for Mammoth Lakes, sightseers going to Yosemite, and a wide variety of other tourists. Located less than 2 miles from the highway, Travertine is an easy stopover for a quick soak.

For the Family

Agua Caliente Hot Springs. A developed hot spring, Agua Caliente is a great place for a bath. The large indoor pool is reserved for adults, but the cooler outdoor pool is open to children. Either one offers a great soaking opportunity in a great location. The spring is run by the County of San Diego within Anza-Borrego Desert State Park in extreme southern California. The park offers unlimited recreation opportunities for the family, including camping, hiking, biking, sightseeing, birding and other animal viewing, history, and archaeology. Plan on visiting the spring during winter when temperatures moderate from the summer highs of 110 to 120 degrees F. The campground and springs are closed from June 1 to September 1.

The Hot Springs

NORTHERN NEVADA

Northern Nevada is one of the most geothermally active portions of the United States. Of the numerous hot springs sprinkled across this part of the state, many have been harnessed for geothermal power. Many more are open for you to discover and enjoy. Because the majority of land in Nevada (80 percent) is controlled by the Bureau of Land Management, Nevada is a great place to go to get away from it all.

Northern Nevada is dominated by ranching and mining. The region is included in a physiographic region termed the Great Basin. The name comes from the fact that all water remains landlocked, never reaching the sea. Most of this water is deposited as ground water, or evaporates away. The region's most distinctive feature is its series of mountain ranges. The ranges all trend north-south, and many reach well over 8,000 feet in elevation. These mountains support completely different plants and animals than the valley floors, lying a few miles away. This varied topography is one of northern Nevada's strong points, allowing travelers a quick escape from the desert heat on the valley floor.

RENO AREA

The Greater Reno area has several hot springs. Some of the springs are on private property, however. Others offer limited bathing opportunities or are tapped completely by geothermal power companies. Before the city reached as far southwest as it does now, there was a collection of natural hot springs near the present-day Moana Lane. The Moana Hot Springs were the site of a large spa which, in the early 1900s, could be reached by streetcar from downtown. Since then, the hot spring waters have been used in individual houses for space heating and in swimming pools.

If you are spending a quick getaway weekend in Reno, gambling, skiing, or just sightseeing, both of the springs listed below are within a short drive of the city.

1

Steamboat Hot Springs

General description: A historic hot springs resort south of Reno immediately off U.S. Highway 395. Closed for years, the resort has recently reopened. Its many large-volume hot springs have provided bathing for centuries, and now support a large geothermal plant across the highway from the present resort.

Location: About 11 miles south of Reno.

Primitive/developed: Developed.

Best time of year: Year-round.

Restrictions: This is a privately owned resort.

Access: Immediately off the highway, this resort can be reached by any vehicle.

Water temperature: Varies depending on room.

Nearby attractions: Reno, Carson City, Mount Rose, Virginia City.

Services: Gas, food, and lodging can be found north and south along US 395.

Camping: None at the resort itself, but there are several Forest Service campgrounds nearby, including Ophir Creek, south on US 395.

Steamboat Hot Springs.

Maps: Nevada Highway Map; USGS Carson City, NV quadrangle (1:100,000 scale).

Finding the springs: From Reno drive south on U.S. Highway 395 about 11 miles. Shortly after passing the intersection with Nevada Highways 341/431 to Virginia City and Mount Rose, keep an eye out for a Mission-style building on the east side (on your left). Turn left onto the paved road leading to the resort. The resort is not well-marked, so keep your eyes open while traveling south.

The hot springs: Steamboat Hot Springs is built on an extremely geo-thermally active hillside. A large geothermal power plant was built recently on

Steamboat Hot Springs

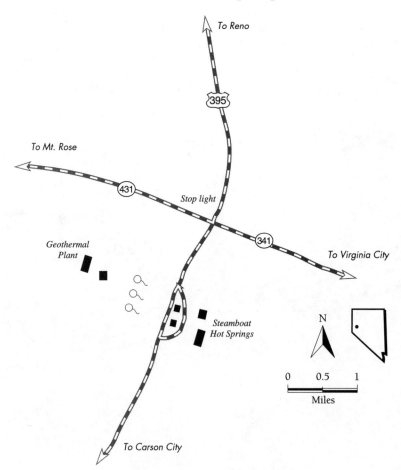

the west side of the highway, tapping the largest portion of the springs in the area. Plenty of hot water remains for the Steamboat resort, however. Its source is enclosed by a cement structure, with steam billowing from it for most of the year. The resort offers a variety of bathing rooms to the public. Temperatures vary in these rooms. Phone ahead at (702) 853-0858 for current rates, hours, and details.

Steamboat history: Located close to emigrant pathways and settlements, these hot springs have been utilized continuously since prehistoric times. During the nineteenth-century westward migration, the hot springs lay on a commonly traveled route from the Truckee Meadows to the Carson Valley and beyond. One of the first hot springs sites to be exploited in the West, Steamboat had a hospital and bathhouse as early as 1860. Felix Monet was the first to develop the springs, acquiring the property in the late 1850s, and building the bathhouse in 1860.

The springs were named because the steam emanating from within sounded like the puffing of a steamboat. With the discovery of vast amounts of silver in the Comstock Lode, and the establishment of Virginia City in the mountains to the east, the resort served as a terminal for the Virginia & Truckee Railroad beginning in 1871. A small town sprang up in the immediate vicinity that included a post office by 1880. Many Virginia City residents visited the fancy hot springs resort. Most notably, the springs were profiled by mining town humorist Mark Twain, in his piece entitled "Curing a Cold." The springs passed through the hands of several owners through the years, their name changing between Reno Hot Springs, Mount Rose Hot Springs, and Radium Hot Springs, among others.

The resort was closed for a time, during which a large geothermal plant was opened on the west side of US 395. The vast amount of energy produced from the hot springs has been utilized in a variety of ways, even providing a flameless source of heat for the manufacture of plastic explosives.

2

Pyramid Lake Hot Springs

General description: A series of hot springs of varying temperatures and flow rates on the north side of an immense desert lake. The springs offer bathing opportunities while the lake offers ample recreation, including swimming, boating, and fishing.

Location: In northern Nevada on the Pyramid Lake Indian Reservation, about 50 miles north of Reno and 50 miles south of Gerlach.

Primitive/developed: Primitive.

Best time of year: Spring, summer, and fall. Roads during the winter can be wet and muddy, and during high lake levels some of the springs may be submerged.

Restrictions: These springs are on the Pyramid Lake Indian Reservation. At times the reservation has closed this area to public access due to overuse and disturbances. A day-use permit must be obtained from the marina in Sutcliffe or at one of the collection points along the road. Purchase a copy of the Pyramid Lake Paiute Tribe Map/Brochure for restrictions and regulations. For more information contact the Pyramid Lake Ranger Station at (702) 476-0132, or the Pyramid Lake Paiute Tribe at (702) 574-1002.

Access: High-clearance vehicles are recommended, since the road to the springs can be difficult. During wet periods you'll need four-wheel drive. Stay on established roads—even four-wheel-drive vehicles can get stuck in the loose sand near the lake.

Water temperature: Varies depending on spring. Temperatures at the well valve average 150 degrees F. Be careful!

Nearby attractions: Pyramid Lake, Reno.

Services: Gas and food can be found in the reservation town of Sutcliffe, 20 miles south.

Camping: Camping is not permitted in the vicinity of the hot springs themselves, but is allowed on other portions of the reservation for a fee. Inquire at the marina store or at the ranger station about locations and current rates.

Maps: Pyramid Lake Paiute Tribe Map/Brochure; USGS Kumiva Peak, NV quadrangle (1:100,000 scale).

Finding the springs: From Reno, take Interstate 80 to Nevada Highway 445 in Sparks. Exit north off I-80 to NV 445 (Pyramid Way) and travel about 28 miles to the intersection of NV 445 and Nevada Highway 446. At this intersection (at the lake), turn left and go 3 miles to the town of Sutcliffe, where you can buy gas, groceries, and use permits. From Sutcliffe continue north on NV 445 for 13 miles (the road becomes dirt eventually). Pass a ranch on your left and look for a relatively well-traveled dirt road on

Pyramid Lake Hot Springs

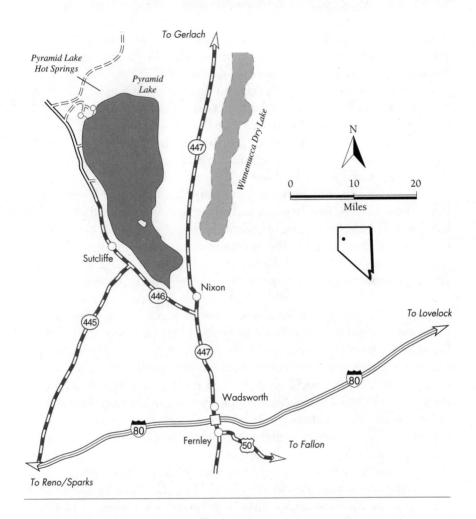

the right. Take this secondary dirt road to the right. This leads to the Needles and Pyramid Lake Hot Springs, and is not usually signed. Travel on this secondary road for about 5 miles; it becomes more sandy as it approaches the lake. The road will eventually lead you directly to the iron valve and well described below.

The hot springs: The main feature of the Pyramid Lake Hot Springs is a large column of steam emanating from an iron valve capping a large well. Hot water drips from this valve at an extremely high temperature, and cools as it flows to the lake. Over the years people have employed various means to trap this hot water into pools before it reaches the lake. Because the soil in this area is fine, most of these pools are short-lived. Even the placing of tarps in the pools has been largely unsuccessful (and just makes an unsightly mess). In warmer months you may enjoy bathing in the lake where the hot spring water enters, providing a slightly warmer environment than the lake water itself. In winter months the lake water is far too cold for this, however.

On the northern shore of Pyramid Lake, the hot springs are in an area termed "The Needles" because of large tufa deposits abounding in and around the springs. These tufa deposits formed when the lake level was higher and spring water mixed with lake water, precipitating the material you see today. These tufa mounds can be seen far from the present-day shoreline of the lake, showing how high the lake level was in the past.

There are other hot springs in the vicinity of the iron valve. These springs have substantially less flow, however, and some may be submerged during higher lake levels. The smaller springs offer little in the way of bathing, but are interesting to look at nevertheless. The area is quite scenic and demands exploration.

This portion of Pyramid Lake has always been a place of magic to the Northern Paiute, who have called it home for thousands of years. Please respect it.

Pyramid Lake's first inhabitants: Although man is known to have inhabited what is now Pyramid Lake as many as 11,000 years ago, the Northern Paiute people who occupy it today arrived around A.D. 1400. Many mysteries surround the early inhabitants of the Pyramid Lake region, but three different cultures probably occupied and abandoned the region before the Northern Paiutes came to stay. Oral traditions of the Pyramid Lake Paiutes hint at these earlier peoples, while archaeological evidence points to their rather complicated culture and society. Excavations in the caves surrounding Pyramid Lake show that these early inhabitants utilized a variety of food sources; made elaborate jewelry, stone effigies, and tools; and painted pictographs on the surrounding rocks.

The Pyramid Lake Paiutes are a band of the Northern Paiutes and call themselves the *Kuyuidokado*, or "fish-eaters." Most other bands of Northern Paiute were also named for the main source of food upon which they depended. The Cui-ui, a native sucker fish, along with the cutthroat trout provided sustenance for the Pyramid Lake Paiutes.

The Pyramid Lake War of 1860: Between Wadsworth and Nixon, Nevada Highway 447 follows the path taken by white settlers in the Carson Valley who, in 1860, came to do battle with the Northern Paiutes living at Pyramid Lake. Not until the Battle of the Little Bighorn in Montana in 1876 did so many whites die in a confrontation with Native Americans.

Although Indian-white relations remained amenable after initial contact

Pyramid Lake Hot Springs.

in Nevada, friction had developed following the appearance of more and more whites in the Paiute homeland. The Paiutes, who saw their way of life threatened, grew weary of the encroachments. They attacked Williams Station on the Carson River on May 7, 1860. Retaliation came with the kidnapping of two Paiute women later in the month. A second attack by nine Paiutes (led by Natchez and Numaga) incited area residents to invade the Paiutes' home base and defeat them once and for all.

Volunteers from all over the region, including Virginia City, Silver City, and Carson City, hastily organized themselves into a ragtag militia and headed for Pyramid Lake on May 10. The 105 settlers were led by Carson Ranger William Ormsby. The volunteer posse camped two nights on its way to Pyramid Lake—one of these campsites can be seen 2.5 miles east of I-80 where it passes through Wadsworth; look across the Truckee River near a stand of cottonwood trees. This area was also a favorite camping spot for emigrant wagon trains. From this campsite the volunteers on May 12 followed a well-marked trail north along the Truckee River and through the area of present-day Nixon.

Spotting a group of Paiutes to the northeast, upslope, a detachment of settlers charged the position. Upon reaching the spot where the Indians were first seen, the volunteer soldiers were surprised to find they had disappeared. Soon thereafter a second group of Paiutes was spotted to the south, putting the men in a dangerous position. The attack began rapidly, with Indians appearing from concealment and pouring bullets and arrows down upon the surprised forces. Within 10 minutes the attack was over, the volunteer posse in complete disarray and making a panicked retreat. The trap had worked.

At a place just south of where the present highway passes through Nixon, another group of Paiutes waited in concealment. Many of the volunteers attempted to avoid this ambush by trying to cross the river, but were repulsed by the swift current. Continuing in their retreat, the settlers were slowed on their climb back uphill to the plateau, the Indians in hot pursuit. Upon reaching the pass, even the rear guard, left to hold the attack, retreated with their comrades. Though an authenticated count of casualties was never made, at least seventy settlers remained unaccounted for, with Ormsby among the dead.

Once word of the "massacre" reached the mining and ranching settlements to the west, a second force was raised, and another attack was planned on the Paiutes. This time volunteers came in from settlements as far away as Sacramento, California. Four companies of regular U.S. Army troops were also enlisted to help, and were brought all the way from San Francisco. On May 24, 1860, this second force marched toward Pyramid Lake. The Paiute defense met up with the army near the site of the previous battle, where many of the dead still lay. Paiute women, children, and noncombatants fled north to safety. The second battle was a stalemate.

On June 4 of the same year a group of white settlers returned to the battle site and found the Indian camp abandoned. The Paiutes' route north followed the west shore of Winnemucca Lake, adjacent to present-day NV 447. The settlers attempted to follow the fleeing Indians, and one scout was killed in the pursuit. Another detachment of regular army troops was sent to the campsite later in the year, setting up a temporary earthwork named Fort Haven. The more substantial Fort Churchill was built on the Carson River later in 1860, giving the area's settlers what they wanted. A peace treaty with the Paiutes was negotiated later in the same year by Colonel Frederick Lander.

BLACK ROCK DESERT

Rich in history, prehistory, natural beauty, and geothermal resources, this part of Nevada is a must-visit for those who enjoy the peaceful solitude only the desert can offer. Only a few hours from the bright lights of Reno, this high desert setting makes you feel as though you're in another world. Near the margins of the Black Rock Desert Playa, most area springs are a 2- to 3-hour drive from Reno. The nearest town is Gerlach, a small railroad town with only the most basic services, including a small hotel and casino.

You will be far from the conveniences of civilization on this trip, so come prepared. Bring more water than you plan to consume, plenty of food, a basic automotive tool kit, a shovel, first-aid supplies, and warm clothing. Also be sure to notify someone of your trip destination, when you plan to leave, and when you plan to return.

The Black Rock Desert rests on the remains of a huge prehistoric lake, Lake Lahonton, which covered a large part of northern Nevada during the Pleistocene Epoch. Ringed by imposing mountain ranges, the area we see today was filled with water as recently as 10,000 years ago. Large animals, all of which are now extinct, roamed this country during the Ice Age. Huge woolly mammoths, saber-toothed cats, ground sloths, and many other animals lived in the region. The first people who lived here hunted these animals. Occasionally evidence of these ancient creatures turns up in the Black Rock Desert, the most notable of which was an intact skeleton of a woolly mammoth found less than ten years ago on the Black Rock Desert Playa.

Most of the land you will cross to get to area hot springs is managed by the Bureau of Land Management. But there are also areas of private property in the region; stay out of these without prior permission. Please remember to stick to established roads, pack out all trash, and leave the desert as you found it.

3

Gerlach Hot Springs

General description: A warm pool owned by the town of Gerlach. The pool, when open, is available for public use and offers showers, changing rooms, and bathrooms. Under construction for years, Gerlach Hot Springs now offers a no-frills bathing experience, perfect for cleaning off your trail dust, then moving on.

Location: In Gerlach, 107 miles north of Reno in northwestern Nevada.

Primitive/developed: Developed.

Best time of year: Year-round.

Restrictions: The pool is owned by the town of Gerlach; there is a $4 fee for day use.

Access: Any vehicle.

Water temperature: About 100 degrees F.

Nearby attractions: Black Rock Desert Playa, Pyramid Lake.

Services: Gas, food, and lodging can be found in Gerlach.

Camping: Camping is not permitted at the springs, but it is allowed on plenty of public land outside of Gerlach, although there are no developed sites.

Map: USGS Gerlach, NV quadrangle (1:100,000 scale).

Finding the springs: From Reno, travel east on Interstate 80 for 35 miles, exiting north onto Nevada Highway 447. Take NV 447 through the town of Wadsworth and go 16 miles to Nixon. Continue north for 56 miles to Gerlach. At the north end of town, Gerlach Hot Springs are immediately off the road on the right.

The hot springs: Completed only recently, this public hot springs pool has been closed for most of its existence and still may be closed at times. During periods of closure hot showers can still be purchased for $3; these can be a welcome luxury if you have been collecting dust for the past few days. Immediately outside the town of Gerlach, the facility is built adjacent to the Great Boiling Hot Springs (see below) and offers a nice bathing opportunity on your way to or from points beyond. Toilets and showers are also available. The phone number for the pool is (702) 557-2220.

Gerlach Hot Springs, Great Boiling Hot Springs, Trego Hot Spring, Jackson Mountain Hot Spring

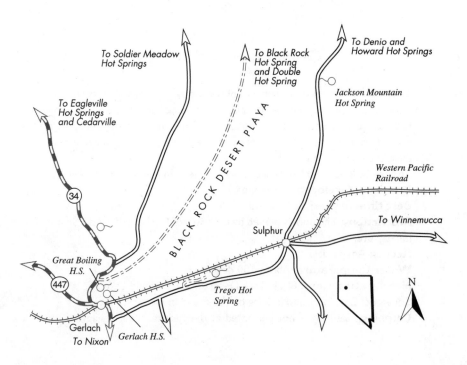

4

Great Boiling Hot Springs

General description: A once-active hot springs resort outside the town of Gerlach. Several large pools of blue and green water with telltale steam have greeted visitors to the area for years. Although owners of the property have recently closed the springs to bathing and camping, the springs themselves are still worth seeing.

Location: Immediately outside Gerlach in northern Nevada, 107 miles north of Reno.

Primitive/developed: Primitive, although once a developed resort.

Best time of year: Year-round.

Restrictions: The property owners have closed the springs to bathing and camping, although they usually don't mind if you just take a look. But ask first, and be aware that these restrictions may change in the future, becoming either more lax or more strict. Be sure to obey any posted signs.

Access: Just about any car can make the short drive on a dirt road off the state highway.

Water temperature: At the main source the water is as hot as 150 degrees F. (be careful!); the other main pool is about 110 degrees F.

Nearby attractions: Black Rock Desert Playa, Pyramid Lake.

Services: Gas, food, and lodging can be found in Gerlach, immediately south of the springs.

Camping: Camping is not allowed at the springs, although there is plenty of public land nearby where camping is permitted. There are no developed sites in the area, however.

Map: USGS Gerlach, NV quadrangle (1:100,000 scale).

Finding the springs: From Reno travel east on Interstate 80 for 35 miles, exiting onto Nevada Highway 447 north. Take NV 447 through the town of Wadsworth and go 16 miles to Nixon. Continue north for 56 miles to Gerlach. At the north end of the town, pass Gerlach Hot Springs; soon thereafter you will see the remains of a building immediately off the road on the right. Take the short dirt road leading to the building and the springs.

The hot springs: This is one of the largest hot springs in the area, and for that reason was made into a resort several decades ago. Even after the resort closed down, people continued to use the springs for bathing and camping. Recently, however, due to vandalism and other factors, the springs have been closed to the public. The several original bathhouses have all but collapsed today. There are two main pools, with several hot water sources. The main source

Great Boiling Hot Springs.

of water is hotter than 150 degrees F. and is fenced off to keep people from injuring themselves. A nineteen-year-old woman was killed in this portion of the springs in 1973. The second pool has steps leading into it, which once made for excellent bathing opportunities. Unfortunately, careless people have continued to leave trash and vandalize the area. Perhaps one day these springs will be open to bathing again.

There are several other hot springs in the immediate vicinity of Great Boiling Hot Springs, the only bathable one being utilized by Gerlach Hot Springs. Several mud volcanoes surrounding Great Boiling Hot Springs reportedly erupt on occasion. These mud volcanoes consist of hot spring water immediately below the surface, covered by mud; the heated water erupts much like that of a geyser would, through a narrow vent. Mud is often spewed great distances during these rare eruptions.

John Charles Frémont—The Pathfinder: During his historic mapping expedition of 1843-1844, Captain John Charles Frémont of the U.S. Topographic Corps camped at this spring. Frémont and his party were exploring the Great Basin, searching for the source of the legendary San Buenaventura River. The maps and descriptions of the country in which they traveled would be utilized by hundreds of later emigrants to California and Oregon. Frémont described the hot springs as "the most extraordinary locality of hot springs we had met during the journey," and recorded temperatures as high as 208 degrees F. The explorers had been away from home for over a year when they reached the hot spring, after which they traveled south to Pyramid Lake. As with many other places throughout the west, Frémont gave the hot springs their name. Frémont also named Pyramid Lake—the small triangular island near the south shore reminded him of the great edifices in Egypt.

5

Trego Hot Spring

(See map on page 22.)

General description: About 4 hours from Reno, Trego Hot Spring consists of a small, shallow, silty, warm-source pond that flows into a ditch and subsequently cools. The spring lies on the edge of the Black Rock Desert Playa, adjacent to the Western Pacific Railroad. Visiting this spring makes for an excellent camping trip, and can be linked to other trips listed in this book.
Location: Northwestern Nevada, about 120 miles north of Reno.
Primitive/developed: Primitive.
Best time of year: Spring or fall. During winter, roads can be muddy and impassable for passenger cars. The area can be hot in summer.
Restrictions: None.
Water temperature: 100 degrees F. at the source (at the railroad tracks); about 95 degrees F. in the pond, and cooler in the ditch.
Access: During dry periods most passenger cars can make the trip. If roads are wet, four-wheel drive is mandatory.
Nearby attractions: Black Rock Desert Playa, Pyramid Lake.
Services: None, the nearest gasoline, food, and lodging is in Gerlach, about 20 miles south.
Camping: Plenty of undeveloped space near the spring.
Map: USGS Gerlach, NV quadrangle (1:100,000 scale).
Finding the spring: From Reno, take Interstate 80 east 35 miles, exiting onto Nevada Highway 447 north. Travel on NV 447 through Wadsworth and go 16 miles to Nixon. Immediately north of Nixon on NV 447 is Pyramid Lake. Continue north on NV 447 for 56 miles to Gerlach, where you will want to gas up if you plan on being out for more than the day. From the only gas station in town (Bruno's Texaco), backtrack on NV 447 across

the dry lakebed for 2.7 miles to the first dirt road on your left. Take this graded road east for 15.6 miles to a secondary dirt road, also on your left. Take this road about 1 mile to the spring.

The hot spring: Trego Hot Spring consists of a small pond adjacent to the spring's source. The pond is 2 to 3 feet deep, with a silty bottom in which you'll sink to above your ankles. The clear water is about 100 degrees F. at the source. The water flows out of the pond and into a ditch, with its temperature decreasing the farther it gets from the pond. Depending upon the time of year you visit, you may want to sample each part of this spring to find the right temperature to suit your desires.

The Nobles Trail: Trego Hot Spring was a campsite along the emigrant trail known as Nobles Cut-off, used during the early 1850s. Beginning in 1847 the Applegate Trail diverted from the main emigrant trail at Lassen's Meadows on the Humboldt River (near present-day Rye Patch Reservoir), traveling west to Rabbithole Springs, then north across the Black Rock Desert. Traveling along the western edge of the Black Rock Range, the trail headed west again at Soldier Meadows through High Rock Canyon, eventually reaching Oregon. Prominent landowner and explorer Peter Lassen blazed a divergent trail off this trail

Trego Hot Spring.

near Goose Lake south to his ranch in northern California. Lassen's Trail, far from a shortcut to California, actually led travelers 200 miles out of the way from the more heavily traveled Truckee and Carson river routes. The Nobles Trail was a shortcut off the much longer Lassen/Applegate Trail, and was used for the first time in 1852. In 1853, the trail changed its course slightly and passed by what is now known as Trego Hot Spring and the town of Gerlach.

6

Jackson Mountain Hot Spring

(See map on page 22.)

General description: In an equally scenic setting to that of Trego Hot Spring, this hot spring also lies on the east side of the Black Rock Desert Playa.

Location: In northwestern Nevada, about 40 miles northeast of Trego Hot Spring. The spring is about 2 hours northwest of Winnemucca by a different road (see map) or about 160 miles northeast of Reno.

Primitive/developed: Primitive.

Best time of year: Spring and fall. Roads can become more difficult during wet winters, and summers can be hot.

Restrictions: None.

Access: When the roads are dry, most passenger vehicles can make the trip. But a high-clearance vehicle is recommended, and a four-wheel drive is necessary when the road becomes wet or washed out.

Water temperature: 110 degrees F. at the source.

Nearby attractions: Black Rock Desert Playa, the old railroad townsite of Sulphur.

Services: None; the nearest gasoline, food, and lodging is in Winnemucca, 68 miles southeast, or Gerlach, about 50 miles southwest.

Camping: Undeveloped space for a few vehicles near the springs, and plenty of open space in the immediate vicinity.

Map: USGS Jackson Mountains, NV quadrangle (1:100,000 scale).

Finding the springs: Follow directions (above) from Reno to Gerlach. From Gerlach, travel south on Nevada Highway 447 for 2.7 miles to a graded dirt road on your left (the same road you would take to get to Trego Hot Springs). Take this road for 41 miles to the old railroad town of Sulphur. Turn left (north) out of Sulphur, crossing the railroad tracks on a graded dirt road marked by a sign for Denio. Take this road 11 miles to find the hot spring on your right, directly off the road. To reach Winnemucca, continue on the main graded road straight through Sulphur instead of turning left to Jackson Mountain Hot Spring.

The hot spring: Jackson Mountain Hot Spring consists of a small source of hot water atop a ridge of travertine. The source (about 110 degrees F) trickles down the ridge into a small pool and eventually into a small pond. At one time this pond may have offered bathing opportunities, but at present it serves more as a watering trough for cattle. Perhaps some dedicated volunteers may one day improve part of the spring enough to offer a soak. The breathtaking scenery of the Black Rock Desert makes up for the more limited bathing opportunities.

Prehistoric inhabitants: Native Americans have inhabited the Black Rock Desert area as far back as 10,000 years, and as recently as 150 years ago. Several bands of Northern Paiutes called the Black Rock Desert home within the past two centuries. The springs found in several places around the lake were no doubt a source of reliable water for these native people.

Evidence for prehistoric occupation of the Jackson Mountain Hot Spring can be found if one looks closely. In the area immediately surrounding the spring, small pieces of a rock known as chert can be found. Hundreds of these

Jackson Mountain Hot Spring.

rocks are what archaeologists call "flakes." The broken edges of this material are very sharp, and made excellent tools such as spear points, hide scrapers, choppers, and other implements. Remember that these flakes are archaeological resources and should not be taken from their place. The hot spring is on federal land and the removal of artifacts is a crime. Leave these resources for generations to come, so that they, too, can get a glimpse of our prehistoric predecessors.

7

Black Rock Hot Spring

General description: An immense pool of aqua-blue water on the northern reaches of the Black Rock Desert. The spring is incredibly hot, and all precautions should be taken to avoid serious injury.

Location: In Northern Nevada, about 30 miles north of Gerlach.

Primitive/developed: Primitive.

Best time of year: The spring can only be reached when the playa is completely dry. This will usually be during the months of August, September, and part of October. Do not under, any circumstances, try to get there when there is standing water on the playa, or it is wet in any way.

Restrictions: None.

Access: A high-clearance vehicle is necessary, since the last few hundred yards to the spring are a little rough. There is substantial sand at the margins of the playa, so four-wheel drive is best. **No vehicle can make the trip if the playa is wet**; vehicles have become stuck for days in its sticky surface. The sink of the Quinn River is east of where you will be driving, so don't veer off the track. Inquire in Gerlach for conditions on the playa immediately prior to venturing out on its surface.

Water temperature: 150 degrees F. at source, cooling as the water flows away.

Nearby attractions: Black Rock Desert Playa.

Services: None; the nearest gasoline, food, and lodging can be found in Gerlach, about 30 miles away.

Camping: Camping is permitted, but be sure to come prepared since there are no services of any kind at this remote location.

Map: USGS Gerlach, NV quadrangle (1:100,000 scale).

Finding the spring: From Gerlach, travel northwest out of town on Washoe County Road 34. As the road bends north around the playa, keep an eye out for a dirt road marked by two stone pillars. This road will be on your right, about 3 miles after leaving Gerlach. Turn onto this dirt road and drive a few hundred yards onto the playa surface. You will then see tire tracks leading north farther onto the dry lake. Follow these tracks in a northerly direction, staying on the most distinct path.

As you travel north you will see the large, black rock from which the desert derives its name. Head toward this rock, following tracks that lead you in that general direction. Do not stray from the tracks. The drive across the playa is about 25 miles. As the tracks leave the playa on the north side, immediately below the black rock, they continue through hummocky terrain to the hot spring itself.

The hot spring: Another campsite along the Lassen, Applegate, and Nobles trails, Black Rock Hot Spring is a wonder of the region. The spring itself is a massive pool extending to unknown depths. This water is extremely hot, so take all precautions and keep a close hold on children and pets. An emigrant party in the 1850s was unable to stop one of their dogs from jumping in, and the dog was boiled to death in a matter of minutes. A shepherd's wagon lies adjacent to the spring, which some people have covered with tarp for protection from the sun. Although the spring itself is extremely hot, the water does

Black Rock Hot Spring, Double Hot Spring

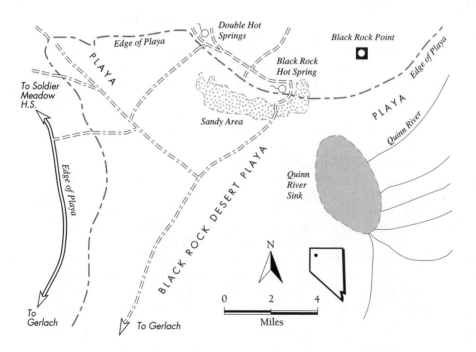

Black Rock Hot Spring.

flow out onto a small marshy area where the water cools off considerably.

Black Rock Hot Spring is far from civilization and can only be reached a few months of the year. Getting there requires following little more than tire tracks. The spring nevertheless—or because of these factors—is a fantastic place to visit. The entire Black Rock Desert spreads out before you, and the brilliant water dazzles your eyes. Be sure to plan ahead for the trip, and inquire locally about playa conditions before you depart.

8

Double Hot Spring

(See map on page 30.)

General description: Another fantastic hot spring on the margins of the Black Rock Desert Playa, even farther away than Black Rock Hot Spring and more difficult to reach. The spring does, however, offer ample bathing opportunities.
Location: In northern Nevada, in the Black Rock Desert about 35 miles north of Gerlach.
Primitive/developed: Primitive.
Best time of year: The spring is best accessed from Black Rock Hot Spring (see above), and therefore should only be visited in August, September, and part of October.
Restrictions: None.
Access: Four-wheel drive may be required. The road from Black Rock Hot Spring to Double Hot Spring can be difficult.
Water temperature: 140 degrees F. at source, cooling to varying temperatures. Some reports place the temperature of the hottest portions of the spring as high as 202 degrees F.
Nearby attractions: Black Rock Desert Playa.
Services: None; the nearest gasoline, food, and lodging can be found in Gerlach, 35 miles away.
Camping: Camping is permitted, but come prepared since there are absolutely no services of any kind and you will be a long drive from civilization.
Map: USGS High Rock Canyon, NV quadrangle (1:100,000 scale).
Finding the spring: From Black Rock Hot Spring, continue on the same road northwest, roughly paralleling the edge of the playa. Follow this increasingly difficult road about 5 miles to another expanse of dark green vegetation, which marks the location of Double Hot Springs.

The hot spring: Similar to Black Rock Hot Spring, Double Hot Spring also has an extremely hot source of which travelers should be wary. There are also numerous seeps in the surrounding area, making the area rather marshy. Explore the entire area to find a place to bathe, but be careful around the hot water.

Evidence for prehistoric occupation of this site abounds. As you will quickly realize, however, modern people have also been visiting this spring for generations—judging by the garbage left by different groups. Older refuse can

Double Hot Spring.

be discerned among more recent debris. As always, do not leave any garbage yourself, and refrain from removing any artifacts from the area.

There are several other hot springs in the immediate area, although none provide any real bathing opportunities. Almost without exception, these springs lie along a geological fault line running roughly north/northwest to south/southeast, along the base of the Black Rock Range to the Trego Hot Spring area. This fault also extends into the Soldier Meadow region, where there are several other hot springs (see below), making the fault about 35 miles long. An 1936 earthquake of 4.1 magnitude was attributed to this fault line.

9

Soldier Meadow Hot Springs

General description: A series of hot springs ponds formed by several seeps in a remote desert setting These hot springs are in an extremely geothermally active valley, offering several choices within a short radius.
Location: In northwestern Nevada, about 60 miles northwest of Gerlach and 170 miles from Reno.
Primitive/developed: Primitive.
Best time of year: Spring, winter, and fall. Summers can be hot.
Restrictions: None.
Access: The trip is best made in a high-clearance vehicle, although some vans and passenger cars can make it. During wet periods you may need four-wheel drive. The road is of varying quality and can be washed out in places, making for sandy spots. In winter and spring the secondary roads can become rather muddy.
Water temperature: Ranging from 100 to 115 degrees F. depending upon the spring chosen.
Nearby attractions: High Rock Canyon, Black Rock Desert Playa, Summit Lake.
Services: None; the nearest gasoline, food, and lodging can be found in Gerlach, 60 miles away. A nearby guest ranch can provide a place to stay, but these springs are best enjoyed by camping adjacent to them.
Camping: Plenty of undeveloped space to camp. Remember to camp away from the springs themselves and respect other people's privacy.
Map: USGS High Rock Canyon, NV quadrangle (1:100,000 scale).
Finding the springs: From Gerlach travel north through town on Nevada Highway 447 until you come to a fork in the road just outside town. (You'll pass Gerlach Hot Spring on your right.) Take the right fork, which is Washoe County Road 34. Travel north on CR 34 along the west side of the Black Rock Desert Playa (after passing Great Boiling Hot Spring on your right) for 12.2 miles. Turn right onto a dirt road with a sign for Soldier Meadow Guest Ranch.

Stay on this main dirt road 43.3 miles until it forks, with a sign pointing towards the Soldier Meadow Guest Ranch. Take the left fork; you will immediately be met with a choice of three roads. From this intersection, take the middle road, which is the least developed of the three choices. There will be some springs seeping onto the road, sometimes making it wet and muddy. Follow this road about 0.6 mile, crossing another road, until you come to a small hill. Continue on the same road up and around

Soldier Meadow Hot Springs, Soldier Meadow Warm Pond

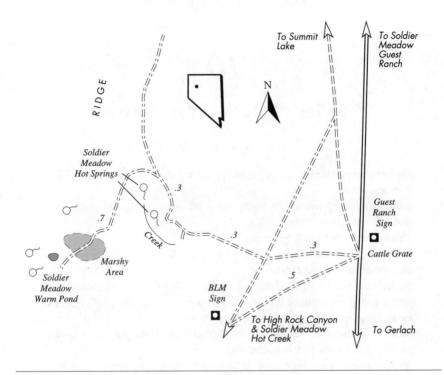

this hill for another 0.3 mile until you spot the hot water seeps on the other side. Park here and select the pond that you prefer.

The hot springs: Settled in a small valley, these springs have a view of the Soldier Meadow area and the majestic Black Rock Range to the east, usually snowcapped in winter. The pond offering the best soaking opportunity is about 5 feet by 5 feet and about 4 feet deep with clear water and a sandy bottom surrounded by reeds. Other ponds nearby (within 50 yards) are hotter and shallower but also can provide a good soak. Be sure to check the temperature before getting in.

Camping is permitted and ideal at this location. There are more than fifty distinct hot springs in this geothermally active valley. Most of these springs are large in volume and temperature, although there are few bathing opportunities.

The valley in which these hot springs are found was named for soldiers stationed at an army post established in the early 1860s. The camp was established deep in the heart of Northern Paiute territory during heightened Indian-white conflict during and immediately after the Civil War.

10

Soldier Meadow Warm Pond

(See map on page 35.)

General description: A large, warm, 5-foot deep pond in the Soldier Meadow area.

Location: Northwestern Nevada, about 60 miles northwest of Gerlach and 160 miles from Reno.

Primitive/developed: Primitive.

Best time of year: Spring and fall. Roads can be wet and muddy in winter, and summers can be hot.

Restrictions: The nearby guest ranch asks that you do not camp at the warm spring itself; please honor that request. There is plenty of undeveloped camping in the immediate vicinity, however.

Access: High-clearance vehicles are needed most of the year. During wet periods you'll want four-wheel drive.

Water temperature: About 95 degrees F., depending upon which part of the pond you are in. In places along the margins of the pond extremely hot water bubbles up through the mud, so be careful!

Nearby attractions: High Rock Canyon, Black Rock Desert Playa, Summit Lake.

Services: None; the nearest gasoline, food, and lodging can be found in Gerlach, 60 miles away.

Camping: No camping allowed at the warm spring itself. There are plenty of other springs nearby where camping is permitted; just remember to camp at a distance from the water and respect other people's privacy.

Map: USGS High Rock Canyon, NV quadrangle (1:100,000 scale).

Finding the spring: From Soldier Meadow Hot Spring (Site 9, above) continue on the road that took you to the spring, traveling in the same direction. Follow the road around to the other side of the creek formed by the hot spring seeps until it meets up with another road. Take this road left and go about 0.5 mile to a large parking and horse tie-up area adjacent to the warm pond. This road is usually wet in places, with the many hot seeps in the area. Tread carefully.

Soldier Meadow Warm Pond.

The hot spring: The warm pond is about 30 by 30 feet and 5 feet deep in the deepest part. The water is approximately 95 degrees F, varying in temperature depending upon where you are in the pond. The Soldier Meadow area is geothermally active, and there are a number of nearby hot springs. Aside from the other two springs described in this vicinity (Springs 9 and 11), the other springs offer limited bathing opportunities due to lack of depth or excessive temperatures. Camping is not permitted at this spot; the local guest ranch asks that you camp at one of the many other hot springs in the area.

11

Soldier Meadow Hot Creek

General description: Similar in setting to other nearby springs, this site offers additional bathing opportunities, with quite a variance in temperatures. The hot creek is only a few miles from Springs 9 and 10, and all can easily be visited in a day.

Location: Northwestern Nevada, about 65 miles northwest of Gerlach and 165 miles from Reno.

Primitive/developed: Primitive.

Best time of year: Spring and fall. Roads can be wet and muddy in winter, and summer can be hot.

Restrictions: None.

Access: High-clearance vehicles required for most of the year. During wet periods you may need four-wheel drive.

Soldier Meadow Hot Creek

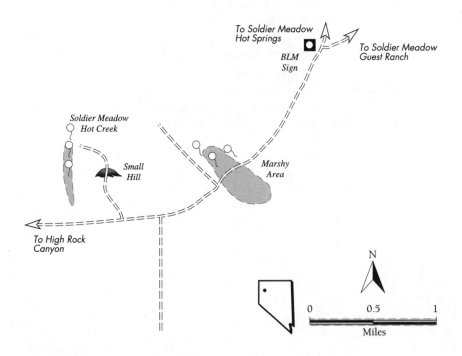

To Soldier Meadow Hot Springs

BLM Sign

To Soldier Meadow Guest Ranch

Soldier Meadow Hot Creek

Small Hill

Marshy Area

To High Rock Canyon

N

0   0.5   1

Miles

Water temperature: Varies; it is generally around 105 degrees F.

Nearby attractions: High Rock Canyon, Black Rock Desert Playa, Summit Lake.

Services: None; the nearest gasoline, food, and lodging can be found in Gerlach, 65 miles away.

Camping: Plenty of undeveloped space. Just remember to camp away from the springs themselves, and respect other people's privacy.

Map: USGS High Rock Canyon, NV quadrangle (1:100,000 scale).

Finding the springs: From Gerlach, proceed north through town on Nevada Highway 447. At the fork in the road out of town, take the right fork, which is Washoe County Highway 34. Proceed north on CR 34 for 12.2 miles to a dirt road on the right, marked with signs to the Soldier Meadow Guest Ranch. Take this road 43.3 miles to a fork in the road with a sign to the Soldier Meadow Guest Ranch. Take the left fork; you will be met immediately with a choice of three roads. Take the road on the left, and follow this road for 0.5 mile to a BLM sign indicating the road to High Rock Canyon and Lake. Bear left at this intersection and continue another 2 miles or so, where you will take a road off to the right. Follow this less developed road uphill about 0.8 mile until you come to a small, green valley where several hot springs form a pleasant creek.

The hot springs: The bright green oasis formed by the springs in this area is an abrupt change from the stark, drab surrounding desert. Several pools have been formed by individuals building dams in the creek where hot water emerges from the ground. These pools vary in depth and temperature, ranging from 90 to 105 degrees F. Many of the springs offer a natural hydrotherapy as the hot creek water flows through the ponds. Located on BLM land, the springs site is open to camping—be sure to camp a fair distance from the creek and pack out whatever you pack in. Do not wash dishes, or yourself, in the creek.

High Rock Canyon historic passageway: Along the Applegate and Lassen trails, the Soldier Meadow region was undoubtedly a welcome campsite for weary emigrants. Beyond the hot creek described above, the trails entered narrow, perilous High Rock Canyon on its way to Massacre Lake and the Surprise Valley. A few emigrants of the 1850s left behind reminders of their passage on the walls of the great canyon. A traveler from Wisconsin left the most well-preserved inscription: "George N. Jaquith July The 16th 1852 from WIS." This historic graffiti can still be clearly read on the wall of High Rock Canyon. To reach the canyon, continue west on the secondary road past the turnoff for the hot creek, into the mountains. A BLM sign will point the way once you reach High Rock Lake. The road through High Rock Canyon is one of the most difficult roads in this book, however, and should only be tried by those

Soldier Meadow Hot Creek.

familiar with off-road driving, in a proper vehicle. You will need substantial clearance and four-wheel drive. Prepare for the worst on this drive, bringing along plenty of provisions and notifying someone of your trip.

DENIO REGION

Near the Black Rock Desert lies a region that is almost as geothermally active and is closely related, geologically. Perhaps even more remote than the Black Rock area, the Denio region beckons desert travelers. Its only town is Denio Junction, a few short miles from the Oregon border. This hamlet has one gas station-restaurant-motel and a small airstrip. The region has changed little over time, and cattle ranching remains Denio's largest industry. Most land in this area is managed by the Bureau of Land Management, and is open to your enjoyment and exploration.

The main road through the area is Nevada Highway 140, which connects points in southern Oregon with U.S. Highway 95 and Winnemucca. Sheldon National Wildlife Refuge borders the region on the west, offering an abundance of wildlife.

The Denio region receives slightly more water than the Black Rock Desert region, and has several small lakes in the mountains near the Oregon border. The region also contains the headwaters of several creeks and watersheds. The Quinn River, which eventually disappears in the Black Rock Desert Playa, emerges from the mountains east of Denio, draining a substantial portion of the area.

12

Baltazor Hot Springs

(See map on page 43.)

General description: These are medium-sized hot springs with several seeps, adjacent to a small, isolated homestead. Although there is limited bathing, a nearby hot spring (Spring 13, The Bog) provides one of the best natural baths in the state.
Location: Extreme northwestern Nevada, about 270 miles northeast of Reno.
Primitive/developed: Primitive.
Best time of year: Year-round.
Restrictions: None.
Access: Most passenger cars can make the trip.
Water temperature: Varies from 130 to 150 degrees F. depending upon the spring or seep. At the hottest portion of the largest source, temperatures of 200 degrees F. have been reported.
Nearby attractions: Sheldon National Wildlife Refuge.
Services: None; gasoline, food, and lodging can be found in Denio Junction, about 4.8 miles away.
Camping: Plenty of undeveloped space at the spring. The spring is immediately off the highway, however, so it offers little privacy.
Map: USGS Denio, NV quadrangle (1:100,000 scale).
Finding the spring: From Denio Junction, travel west on Nevada Highway 140 for 4.8 miles. On your left you will see an abandoned building and grassy field. Turn off the highway at the road to the ruins, and drive a hundred yards or so. Small seeps can be found to the left of the structure; they eventually feed into the grassy fields. To reach the largest hot spring, follow a faint road past the ruins for 0.4 mile to its end in a field, where you will see the spring itself. Do not drive into the spring! The road is a little rough, especially when wet, but it's short enough to walk if your vehicle can't handle it.

Baltazor Hot Springs.

The hot spring: At the edge of a mostly dry lake, these hot springs at one time watered grasses that supported large numbers of cattle. A small, hand-built home lies in partial ruins adjacent to the springs, obviously used for a variety of purposes.

The larger of the two hot springs is hot, 150 to 200 degrees F. DO NOT GO IN! The water from this large spring flows out toward the grassy fields, however, and can be diverted to cool for bathing. The other, smaller seeps here are cooler and also flow toward the field; they too could be diverted for soaking. Be careful, because these waters are hot! In addition, please do not litter, damage, remove objects from, or otherwise vandalize the nearby homestead. The structure itself is most likely private property, and will undoubtedly be fenced off if problems arise.

13

The Bog

General description: A fantastic hot pond formed by hot spring water flowing down a small creek, creating a natural Jacuzzi effect.

Location: Extreme northwestern Nevada, about 280 miles northeast of Reno.

Primitive/developed: Primitive, except for channelization of the creek.

Best time of year: Year-round.

Restrictions: None.

Access: Most passenger cars can make the trip.

Water Temperature: About 105 degrees F. in the pond.

Nearby attractions: Sheldon National Wildlife Refuge.

Services: None; gasoline, food, and lodging can be found in Denio Junction, 14 miles away.

Camping: Plenty of undeveloped space. Just remember to camp away from the springs themselves, and respect other people's privacy.

Map: USGS Denio, NV quadrangle (1:100,000 scale).

Baltazor Hot Springs, The Bog, Bog Warm Springs

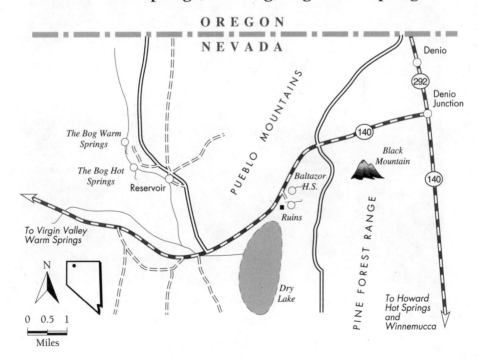

43

Finding the spring: From Denio Junction, travel west on Nevada Highway 140 for about 9.2 miles to a graded dirt road on your right. The dirt road will be immediately after you pass the edge of a hill, on the north side of the highway—you will not have much notice. Drive north for 4.2 miles on the dirt road past a reservoir and ranch until you come to a secondary road on your left. Turn left (west) on this smaller road and drive 100 to 200 yards to the hot springs ditch and pond.

The hot spring: The Bog was formed from the channelization of hot spring water, forming a small pond. The hot water rushes through a culvert from the channel into the pond, forming a Jacuzzi effect. Different portions of the pond are different temperatures, although it's generally about 105 degrees F. The pond ranges in depth from 2 to 4 feet, with a sandy and somewhat mossy bottom. You can park immediately adjacent to the pond itself. Be sure to leave no trash behind.

The spring has been used for more than a century for stock watering, and it supplies water for growing hay. The springs also see domestic use, including mineral baths at the Bog Hot Springs Ranch downstream from the pond described here.

Bog Warm Springs.

14

Bog Warm Springs

(See map on page 43.)

General description: A series of geothermal seeps upstream from The Bog.
Location: Extreme northwestern Nevada, about 280 miles northeast of Reno.
Primitive/developed: Primitive.
Best time of year: Year-round.
Restrictions: None.
Access: Most passenger cars can make the trip.
Water temperature: Varies from 90 to 110 degrees F.
Nearby attractions: Sheldon National Wildlife Refuge.
Services: None; gasoline, food, and lodging can be found in Denio Junction, 14 miles away.
Camping: Plenty. Just remember to camp a few hundred yards away from the springs themselves, and respect other people's privacy.
Map: USGS Denio, NV quadrangle (1:100,000 scale).
Finding the springs: Follow directions to Spring 13, The Bog. From the wide parking area at The Bog, take a smaller dirt road north; it's on your right when you face The Bog. This road is a little rough, so those with passenger cars may opt to walk the short distance. Continue on this dirt road about 0.5 mile, following the creek on the left. After 0.5 mile look for numerous seeps of hot water in the creek; there are few pools.

The hot springs: These warm and hot springs are source waters for The Bog downstream. They vary widely in temperature, so explore the area to find the heat level you desire. As always, be extremely careful and test the water before getting in. You may also need to be creative in your choice of bathing spots, since there are no well-defined pools. Most of the spring water flows down the creek in a wide, shallow channel. If you are really ambitious, you may want to make a small dam and create a makeshift pond. These springs can offer privacy when The Bog is occupied.

15

Virgin Valley Warm Spring

General description: A manmade pool fed by natural hot spring water at a relatively popular campground.
Location: Northwestern Nevada, about 250 miles northeast of Reno.
Primitive/developed: Minimally developed.
Best time of year: Year-round.
Restrictions: Bathing suits required.
Access: Most passenger cars can make the trip.
Water temperature: Varies within the pond, although it averages 90 degrees F.
Nearby attractions: Sheldon National Wildlife Refuge.
Services: None; the nearest gasoline, food, and lodging can be found in Denio Junction, 28 miles away.
Camping: A state campground at the spring allows free camping. The

Virgin Valley Warm Spring

OREGON

To Adel

NEVADA

Sign

Cedarville Road

Flattop Butte

Sign

140 Gorge

To Denio Junction and The Bog H.S.

Ponds

SHELDON NATIONAL WILDLIFE REFUTE

Refuge HQ

Pond

Campground

Virgin Valley Warm Spring

N

To Summit Lake and Soldier Meadows

0   0.5   1

Miles

campground has plenty of space, pit toilets, and beautiful scenery location. Camping is not permitted within 50 feet of the warm pond.

Map: USGS Denio, NV quadrangle (1:100,000 scale).

Finding the spring: From Denio Junction travel west on Nevada Highway 140 for 25 miles. Turn left at the sign to Virgin Valley and the Royal Peacock Mine. Take this graded dirt road about 2.7 miles to the campground and warm pond.

The hot spring: The campground at Virgin Valley is a popular destination for outdoor enthusiasts in northern Nevada. Unless you are here on a weekday in the off-season, don't expect to have the place to yourself. A couple of old buildings (one a bathhouse) adjacent to the spring are closed to public use. The warm pond measures about 30 by 30 feet and has a nice sandy bottom. The temperature hovers around 85 to 90 degrees F., depending upon the time of year. A new stone patio and small stepladder make access easier. This pond serves as a welcome oasis to those traveling in the desert backcountry for extended periods, an excellent stopover point. Also visit Baltazor Hot Springs, The Bog, and Bog Warm Springs (Springs 12-14) if you are in this area.

For birders, Sheldon National Wildlife Refuge offers abundant viewing opportunities. The ponds you pass on your way to the campground are generally full of birdlife, often a wide variety of species. In addition, canyons south of the campground also contain reliable water sources and generally support birds and other animals.

Virgin Valley Warm Spring.

16

Howard Hot Spring

General description: A small, crudely formed hot spring pond in isolated northern Nevada. Its small source atop a small sinter hill flows into a shallow pool formed by a makeshift dam.

Location: Northwestern Nevada, about 80 miles northwest of Winnemucca and 275 miles northeast of Reno.

Primitive/developed: Primitive.

Best time of year: Year-round.

Restrictions: None.

Access: Most passenger cars can make the trip. In wet weather you may need four-wheel drive.

Water temperature: At the source the water is 130 degrees F., but it cools to 105 degrees .F at the pond.

Nearby attractions: Sheldon National Wildlife Refuge.

Services: None; the nearest gasoline, food, and lodging can be found in Denio Junction, about 18 miles away.

Camping: Plenty of undeveloped space. Keep your car on established

Howard Hot Spring.

Howard Hot Spring

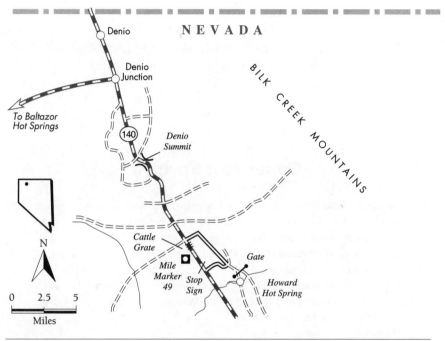

OREGON

NEVADA

Denio

Denio Junction

To Baltazor
Hot Springs

140

Denio
Summit

BILK CREEK MOUNTAINS

N

0   2.5   5
Miles

Cattle
Grate

Mile
Marker
49

Stop
Sign

Gate

Howard
Hot Spring

roads and respect other people's privacy.

Map: USGS Denio, NV quadrangle (1:100,000 scale).

Finding the spring: From Denio Junction, travel south on Nevada 140
for 17 miles, then turn left onto a fairly obvious graded dirt road. Keep an
eye out for this road after crossing a cattleguard near mile marker 49—
watch for a stop sign facing away from the highway. Take the dirt road for
0.6 mile to a smaller dirt road on your right. Take this road 0.1 mile farther, passing through a gate (close it behind you) and immediately meeting
a fork in the road. Take the faint dirt road on your right and follow it about
0.3 mile to the spring.

From Winnemucca, travel north on U.S. Highway 95 for 31 miles to
NV 140. Turn left (northwest) and go 48 miles. Look for the graded dirt
road on your right after the sign "Denio Junction 20 miles."

The hot spring: Howard Hot Spring is one of several in the immediate
area. It's the only one that has been dammed up for bathing, however, and is
open to the public. The water emerges from the side of a small hill and flows
downhill to a place where it has been dammed by volunteers. This pond is

about 8 by 6 feet and about 2 feet deep. The bottom is generally sandy, although it does have a lot of algae, giving the bottom a brownish appearance. Don't be put off by the color or the sediment you will raise when getting in. The water is rather hot, though, and can wear you out in a hurry. The hot spring water eventually flows into a marshy area used by cattle. Other portions of this small hot creek could probably be diverted for additional bathing. Please respect the area by keeping vehicles on the established roads and packing out all trash.

17

Dykes Hot Springs

General description: A series of hot springs flowing into a large, warm pond in isolated northern Nevada. The water has been diverted into an old bathtub in one place, offering a very hot soak.

Location: In northwestern Nevada, about 80 miles northwest of Winnemucca.

Primitive/developed: Only slightly developed. The bathtub has been brought in, and the pond formed by a bulldozer.

Best time of year: Year-round.

Restrictions: None.

Access: Most passenger cars can make the trip. The roads can be muddy in wet weather, and four-wheel drive may be necessary.

Water temperature: 150 degrees F. at the source, about 115 degrees F. in the hot tub, and 80 degrees F. in the pond.

Nearby attractions: Black Rock Desert Playa, Summit Lake.

Services: None; the nearest services are in Denio Junction, 35 miles away.

Camping: Plenty of undeveloped space.

Map: USGS Jackson Mountain, NV quadrangle (1:100,000 scale).

Finding the springs: From Denio Junction, travel south on Nevada Highway 140 for about 26 miles. Turn right onto Big Creek Road, which is a well-maintained, graded road. Go about 6 miles until the road dead-ends at Woodward Road. This also is a fairly well-maintained road, but it can become slippery in wet weather. Turn left here and drive past a ranch at about 2 miles, continuing for another 1 mile to a large turnout on the left side of the road. Park and look for the hot spring seeps immediately off the road.

The hot springs: On the northern margins of the Black Rock Desert, Dykes Hot Springs are much easier to reach from the Howard Hot Spring region and are therefore placed in this section. The hot springs emerging from the ground here are extremely hot.

Dykes Hot Springs

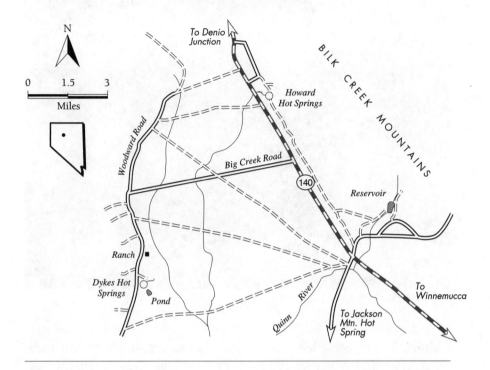

From its sources, the water flows down two separate ravines. When facing the springs from the road, the bathtub is in the ravine on your right. It is hidden from the road and requires a bit of searching to find. The hot water in this tub can also be very hot. To get the right temperature, divert some water into the tub with the pipe provided, and wait for it to cool to the desired temperature. The other ravine has few soaking opportunities, since the water is too hot and has not been diverted or dammed anyplace.

Both ravines flow into a manmade pond used by cattle. This pond is rather murky and not very appealing for swimming. It does have thousands of frogs, which you will undoubtedly hear when you approach. Again, as always, keep your car on established roads and pack out all your trash.

Quinn River region history: Evidence for prehistoric inhabitants abounds in this part of the Black Rock Desert. Archaeological studies and ethnographic information indicate that the first inhabitants of this region were supplanted by the Northern Paiutes about five hundred years ago. The original inhabitants, who may have been here as far back as 9500 B.C., are termed the Lovelock

Dykes Hot Springs.

Culture. These people left clues to their habitation—artifacts, fish traps, petroglyphs, habitation sites, and more. Explorer John Frémont indicated seeing "poor-looking Indians" living in caves on the east side of Pyramid Lake, and unrelated to the Northern Paiutes. Several oral histories also describe another group of Indians living in the Pyramid and Winnemucca Lakes area. These people may have been the last representatives of this earlier culture.

Somewhere in this northern portion of the Black Rock Desert one of the long-standing mysteries of the area took place. Well-known settler Peter Lassen (for whom Mount Lassen and the Lassen Trail were named), along with another man in his party, was killed here in the spring of 1858. One of their party escaped after being wounded, but because the attack was made at night, no one is sure who killed Lassen. Some suspect that it was the Pitt River Indians; others claim it was the work of white men.

Another man gained fame in this region. "Black Rock Tom," a Northern Paiute, was well known for his exploits in raiding and attacking white settlements. Black Rock Tom's white horse was of equal renown, as one source noted:

> All hunters of Indians, who came to an engagement anywhere
> between this and Owyhee, and almost all parties attacked on that
> road, during the past season, remarked, a white horse of extraordi-

nary qualities, the rider of which seemed to take great pride in his efforts to witch the world with noble horsemanship. The white horse was ever spoken of as a wonder of strength and fleetness. His rider, a stalwart Indian, delighted to dally just out of musket range from the white men, caricoling most provokingly, and darting off, occasionally, with the fleetness of the wind.

The rider was Black Rock Tom. During renewed hostilities in the mid-1860s, Black Rock Tom was involved in attacks throughout northern Nevada.

After several raids throughout the Black Rock Desert and Quinn River areas during 1865, several reports of a white horse again surfaced. In September an Indian camp was attacked, some reported seeing "One horse, which had often before attracted notice, was again conspicuous on this occasion—a white animal, that defied all efforts to approach his rider."

One of Black Rock Tom's more infamous attacks was on the road between the Black Rock Desert and Rabbithole Spring. Following this gruesome attack, a party of forty-six soldiers, four volunteer citizens, and eight Paiute guides went after Black Rock Tom's band. During the ensuing battle in the Black Rock Desert, Tom's band was almost completely annihilated. But Black Rock Tom managed to escape. He met his death the next year, however, in the Humboldt Sink near what is now the town of Lovelock.

NORTH-CENTRAL NEVADA

The region bounded on the east and west by portions of the Humboldt National Forest is often referred to as the Owyhee, after the river which drains the area. For the sake of organization, this section covers the Owyhee but also includes hot springs adjacent to Interstate 80 in central Nevada. Most of the area included here served historically as ranching country, supporting nearby mining towns. Paradise Valley, for example, grew up solely as a food supplier to the mining town of Unionville, to the south. Although north-central Nevada has seen considerably more mining than other areas of the state, ranching still remains its dominant activity. Like other parts of northern Nevada, this region is wide open, with thousands of acres to explore. Vast tracts are operated by the Bureau of Land Management, and there are few towns of any substantial size.

Access to the springs described here is easiest from I-80, which borders the region to the south and provides an east-west corridor to Reno and Elko. All manner of services can be found in Winnemucca and Battle Mountain, but come prepared if you plan on venturing far from the highway.

18

Paradise Valley Hot Spring
(Little Humbolt)

General description: A large, travertine-lined pit with extremely hot water, diverted into a plastic tub on the bank of the Little Humboldt River. A wonderful bathing opportunity awaits if water in the tub is allowed to cool.

Location: Northern Nevada, about 50 miles northeast of Winnemucca.

Primitive/developed: Primitive, except for the diversion of water to the plastic tub.

Best time of year: Year-round.

Restrictions: None.

Access: Most passenger cars can make the trip.

Water temperature: 130 degrees F. at source, 115 degrees F. in tub.

Nearby attractions: Historic town of Paradise Valley, Chimney Dam Reservoir.

Services: None; the nearest gasoline, food, and lodging can be found in Winnemucca, 50 miles away. Some services can be found in Paradise Val-

Paradise Valley Hot Spring (Little Humboldt)

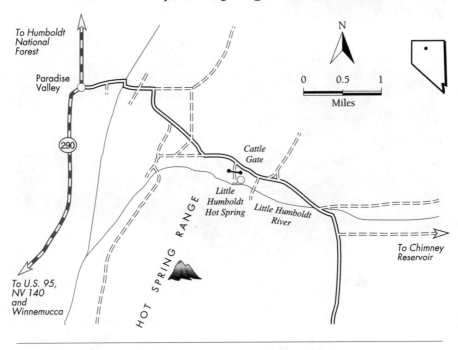

ley, 18 miles away, but do not count on getting supplies in this small farming and ranching center.

Camping: This is private property, and it is unclear as to whether camping is permitted or not at the spring. There is plenty of undeveloped space in the immediate vicinity, however.

Map: USGS Osgood Mountains, NV quadrangle (1:100,000 scale).

Finding the spring: From Winnemucca, travel north on U.S. Highway 95 for 22 miles. Turn onto Nevada Highway 290 northeast for 18 miles to the town of Paradise Valley. Drive through town and turn right (east) beyond the small market, following signs to Chimney Reservoir. Drive on this graded dirt road for 10.6 miles or so (keeping right at a Y in the road), then turn right onto a smaller dirt road with a cattle gate across it. Open the cattle gate, drive through it, and close the gate again behind you. Drive on this dirt road 0.2 mile to the spring.

The hot spring: Water from this large hot spring surrounded by travertine is diverted into a plastic tub. The source is 130 degrees F.—do not go in! Also check the water temperature in the plastic tub before getting in, since it can be extremely hot. This spring is on private property, so please respect all signs and leave no trace of your visit.

Paradise Valley Hot Spring (Little Humboldt).

The town of Paradise Valley is a well-preserved remnant of old Nevada. Chimney Dam Reservoir, east of the hot spring, provides several recreational opportunities. To reach the reservoir, continue on the main road from Paradise Valley for a few more miles.

Paradise Valley history—the 1865 War: Troubles between the Northern Paiutes and non-Indian settlers did not end with the conclusion of the Pyramid Lake War *(see The Pyramid Lake War of 1860, Spring 2)*. Following several isolated conflicts, a band of Paiutes frequenting the Smoke Creek Desert north of Pyramid Lake, led by "Smoke Creek Sam," wreaked havoc on many settlements in this general area. Stage stations and a few individual homesteads were attacked, with several settlers losing their lives. In response to these attacks, Captain A. B. Wells marched with fifty men of the Nevada Volunteers to Winnemucca Lake in 1865. A large group of Northern Paiutes was camping on the shallow lake's shore when Wells attacked. They were not from the Smoke Creek band, however, but were instead Numaga's people, who had not taken part in the recent attacks. Many of the killed were reportedly women, children, and elderly. The actual make-up of the camp is debated even today. No one is quite sure who the Nevada Volunteers fought in March 1865.

In response to this disputed battle, a Paiute war party took revenge on the Granite Creek Station, north of present-day Gerlach. The station remains can still be seen, even though it was burned and its inhabitants killed and mutilated. Afterward, bands of Paiutes along with some Bannocks and Shoshones continued attacking frontier outposts. Many attacks were directed at settlers in the Paradise Valley region, which by this time already boasted a fair-sized town. At an improvised fort on one of the nearby ranches, more than seventy settlers took cover. Eventually the commander of federal troops in Nevada, Colonel Charles McDermitt, sent in more than a hundred soldiers led by Captain Wells. Despite several attempts, these troops were largely ineffective in Paradise Valley and the Paiutes held a vast territory. The Indians attacked settlers from south of the Humboldt River, near Unionville, to as far north as the Quinn and Little Humboldt rivers. The vastly important overland route to California, which passed along the Humboldt along the route of present-day I-80, was in danger of being closed down. Even Colonel McDermitt himself was killed by an Indian war party, in August 1865.

A friendly band of Paiutes at the mining town of Unionville decided to help the local ranchers in their war against the hostile bands of their people. It was under the Indians' competent guiding that army troops were finally able to put an end to the hostilities. The most warlike of the Paiute bands were defeated in the Black Rock Desert region, and put to flight. The last warring band, that of Black Rock Tom (see Spring 17), was also later subdued.

19

Golconda Hot Springs

General description: A collection of hot springs with substantial flow and heat on private property in a small town immediately off Interstate 80. Little or no bathing opportunities.
Location: Within the town of Golconda in northern Nevada, about 16 miles from Winnemucca.
Primitive/developed: Primitive, although surrounded by developed lots.
Best time of year: Year-round.
Restrictions: The spring is on private property, so visitors must obey all signs.
Access: Any vehicle.
Water temperature: About 165 degrees F. at the largest spring, with varying temperatures at the other springs.
Nearby attractions: The historic mining town of Midas.

Services: Gasoline and food can be found in Golconda. The larger town of Winnemucca, about 16 miles away, has all services.

Camping: Camping is not allowed at the springs, but there is plenty of undeveloped public land outside Golconda. Be sure to obey all "no trespassing" signs, however.

Map: USGS Winnemucca, NV quadrangle (1:100,000 scale).

Finding the spring: From Winnemucca, travel east on I-80 for 16 miles to the town of Golconda, and exit the freeway into town. Travel northwest on the main road, then turn right on Morrison Road. Continue over the railroad tracks, where you will take an immediate left on the road paralleling the tracks. The road bends to the right shortly, where you will see the hot springs on your right, in a fenced lot.

The hot springs: Once a famous hot spring resort destination, Golconda Hot Springs are largely unused today. A large hotel and bathhouse at one time serviced hundreds of people, many of whom remained at the springs for weeks at a time. Travelers heading east or west also stopped here to partake of the spa.

The springs are in the middle of the small, roadside town of Golconda. There are several springs within the fenced lot, giving the parcel a bright green color. The springs are on private property, and there is usually a sign stating "no trespassing." If you wish to get closer to the springs, inquire locally for permission to enter the

Golconda Hot Springs.

Golconda Hot Springs

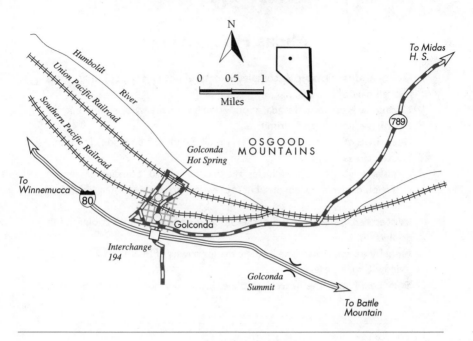

parcel, otherwise KEEP OUT! There is little or no opportunity for bathing at these springs, but they are nonetheless interesting geologic features.

Geologists claim that the springs are related to the enormous Pleistocene Lake Lahonton. The massive prehistoric lake's shoreline reached this location, extending as far north as the Black Rock Desert and as far south as Lovelock. Despite their ancient origin (50,000 years ago), as far as hot springs go, geologists consider these springs to be quite young.

Farmers in the area first put the springs to use in the scalding of hogs. The hot water was also used in growing lettuce, radishes, and onions in this desert location. Beginning in 1940, the hot water was piped into the Golconda tungsten mine, a few miles away.

20

Midas Hot Spring

General description: A completely natural hot spring pool in an uninhabited part of Nevada.
Location: Northern Nevada, about 70 miles northeast of Winnemucca.
Primitive/developed: Primitive.
Best time of year: Spring, summer, or fall. Roads can be muddy in winter.
Restrictions: None.
Access: High-clearance vehicles are recommended. Sturdier passenger cars should have no problems, but four-wheel drive may be needed in wet weather.
Water temperature: 105 degrees F. at the source, a little cooler in the pool itself.
Nearby attractions: The historic mining towns of Midas and Tuscarora, Willow Creek Reservoir.
Services: None; the nearest gasoline, food, and lodging can be found in

Midas Hot Spring

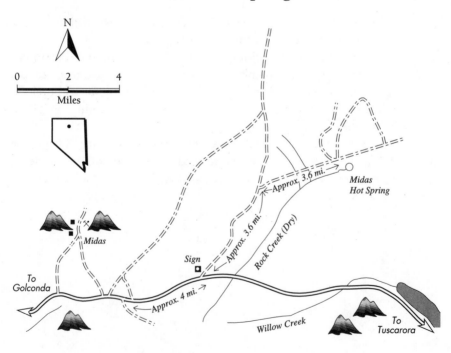

Midas Hot Spring.

Winnemucca, 70 miles away. Limited services (gas and food) can be found in Golconda, 60 miles away.

Camping: There do not appear to be any restrictions against camping near the spring, although it is definitely undeveloped.

Map: USGS Tuscarora, NV quadrangle (1:100,000 scale).

Finding the spring: Travel east of Winnemucca on Interstate 80 for 16 miles to the town of Golconda. From Golconda, take Nevada Highway 789 for about 15.3 miles to where the highway turns to dirt. At the three-way split, follow the main (middle) road with signs leading to Midas. Travel another 27.5 miles to the Midas turnoff. If you want to visit this interesting ghost town, turn left. Otherwise continue straight on the main road to get to the hot spring. Go another 4 miles (from the turnoff to the town of Midas) until you run into a road on your left with signs pointing to Rock Creek. Turn left (north) here and travel 3.6 miles on this less-developed road to another dirt road on your right with a sign indicating Rock Creek. Turn right (east) here and go another 3.6 miles until you reach the hot spring, on your right.

The hot spring: A totally natural hot spring pond, Midas has not been dammed or reinforced, and no such work is necessary for bathing purposes. Unnamed on the topographic map, this spring is located in high desert grazing country, far from civilization. The hot water bubbles up through sand into a small pond about 5 by 5 feet and 4 feet deep. The water is a warm 100 degrees F., pleasant on a cool day but perhaps not quite warm enough on a cold winter day. The water from the spring overflows onto a small plain, where cattle water. The area has the definite imprint of cattle.

Before the cattle came, this spring was obviously used by Native Americans as a small campsite. The spring may have been used as a stopover place or a temporary village site. Evidence for this prehistoric occupation can be seen around the spring. As always, leave any artifacts where you find them.

An interesting side trip can be made to the partial ghost town of Midas. Several houses have been built in the canyon below the site of the mines themselves, with some year-round residents. Further up the canyon, well-preserved remains of Midas's mines can be found immediately off the road. Ore carts, tracks, a mill, and several outbuildings lie largely untouched in this historic canyon. Although mining has continued in adjacent areas, the Midas mines are abandoned today. Midas is one of the best ghost towns in this part of the state, and well deserving of a visit. Please respect all remains by not disturbing them, leaving everything where you found it. In addition, respect the privacy of homeowners in the canyon by not trespassing, obeying all signs, and keeping quiet near the houses.

The equally intriguing and larger ghost town of Tuscarora is east of Midas along the main road from Golconda. Discovered in 1867, with its largest production in the late 1870s, Tuscarora was typical of Nevada mining camps. Remains of several old buildings, a large smokestack, and a plethora of mining artifacts exist here. Tuscarora currently has a post office and a few year-round residents. To reach the town, drive east on the main graded dirt road you took from NV 789, passing turnoffs for Midas and Midas Hot Spring. Follow signs to Willow Creek Reservoir. Stay on the main road past the reservoir for more than 20 miles, following signs to Tuscarora.

21

Carlin Hot Springs

General description: Several springs flowing out of a small hillside in the dry, high desert. A few miles off the interstate, the springs are a little tricky to find but worth a visit.

Location: North-central Nevada, about 5 miles north of Carlin and 28 miles east of Elko.

Primitive/developed: Primitive, except for the diversion of water to a plastic tub.

Best time of year: Fall and spring. Summers can be hot, and roads can be muddy in the winter.

Restrictions: None at the springs themselves. But stay on established roads and close the cattle gate behind you.

Access: High-clearance vehicles are best, although sturdier passenger cars can make the trip. During wet weather you may need four-wheel drive.

Water temperature: 130 degrees F. at source, 110 degrees F. in tub, varying slightly.

Carlin Hot Springs

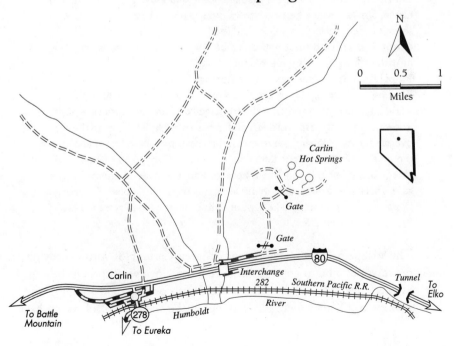

Carlin Hot Springs.

Nearby attractions: Elko, Tuscarora.

Services: None; the nearest gasoline, food, and lodging can be found in Carlin, 5 miles away. The larger town of Elko is about 28 miles away, with several hotels, casinos, gasoline, and food.

Camping: There do not appear to be any restrictions against camping near the spring, but it's undeveloped.

Map: USGS Battle Mountain, NV quadrangle (1:100,000 scale).

Finding the spring: From Carlin, travel east on Interstate 80 to the last Carlin exit. Exit here and take the frontage road on the south side of the freeway, traveling east. Turn left and cross over the freeway at the first overpass. After crossing the freeway, turn right on a paved road and take the first dirt road on your left. You will immediately go through a cattle gate (close it behind you). From here go about 4 miles to another cattle gate. There are several roads in this area; stay on the main one. Go through this second cattle gate and keep your eyes open for green grass indicating the springs in 0.6 mile.

The hot springs: Set in dry grazing country, Carlin Hot Springs provide a welcome splash of vibrant color to the area. There are several springs, but only one has been diverted downhill into a plastic tub or watering trough. People have attempted different methods of trapping the water, most of which have failed. The least effective (and most common) of which are plastic tarps. People have also left substantial amounts of trash at and around the spring, giving it a beat-up look. Beware of the millions of pieces of broken glass. Also beware of the heat of the water in the plastic tub, since the water can often be scalding. If you are willing, you can drain the tub, refill it, remove the water source, and let the water cool before bathing. Although Carlin Hot Spring is not the best bathing opportunity in the book, it makes for a good diversion on trips along I-80.

Carlin–Elko history: Carlin was one of many towns established during the construction of the Central Pacific Railroad across Nevada in 1868-1869. Railroad surveyors laid out lots in the future town of Carlin in December 1869, naming it after Civil War General William P. Carlin, who had served the Union and had seen service in Utah Territory during the 1850s. The town was assured a permanent status (unlike many other railroad towns) when the terminus for the Humboldt Division of the Central Pacific was placed at Carlin. The naming of railroad towns after Civil War generals occurred regularly throughout Nevada, with one notable exception. Superintendent of construction on the Central Pacific line, Charles Crocker apparently wanted to name a town after the elk in the eastern part of the state. He named one of the sites on his route Elko, adding an "o" to make the name sound better.

SOUTH OF INTERSTATE 80

Another largely empty portion of Nevada, the land immediately south of Interstate 80, in the central portion of the state, provides ample opportunities for exploration. The region is also largely controlled by the Bureau of Land Management, but has a higher percentage of mines than the regions previously described. All of the hot springs described here are located on valley floors between the high mountain ranges. For this reason, most are relatively easy to access with a standard vehicle. These hot springs are also primarily in dry settings, and are often oases. Area springs often are used to water stock, though in most cases cattle have been kept out of the springs' sources, maintaining their relatively pristine character. The towns of Winnemucca and Battle Mountain are close to some of these springs, but all are relatively isolated. Look for a private experience here, which can generally be had, but come prepared. As always, let someone know where you're going and when you're expected back.

22

Crescent Valley Hot Springs

General description: Three major and several minor sources of hot water of varying temperature and pool size near a small ranching town. Immediately off the road and adjacent to a few small ranches and houses, one of the springs offers a fairly nice bathing opportunity.

Location: North-central Nevada, about 5 miles east of Crescent Valley and 48 miles southeast of Battle Mountain.

Primitive/developed: Primitive.

Best time of year: Year-round. Summer can be hot, however.

Restrictions: None, but keep your speed down since there are residences within 0.25 mile. Be sure to respect private property.

Access: Most passenger cars can make the trip.

Water temperature: Varies depending upon the spring. Averages 130 degrees F. at the hottest pool, with others ranging between 90 and 100 degrees F.

Crescent Valley Hot Springs

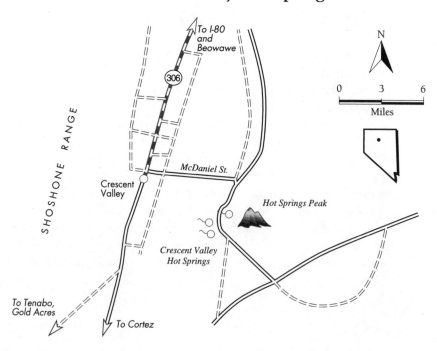

Crescent Valley Hot Springs.

Nearby attractions: Ghost towns of Tenabo, Gold Acres, and Cortez.
Services: None; the nearest gasoline, food, and lodging can be found in Battle Mountain, 48 miles away. There are limited services in Crescent Valley (food, some supplies), but do not count on this small town for your provisioning needs.
Camping: There do not appear to be any restrictions against camping near the springs, but there are no developed campgrounds in the area. Keep in mind that the springs are all right off the road, adjacent to private residences, so this may not be the best place to camp. There is plenty of public land in the surrounding vicinity. Obey any "no trespassing" signs.
Map: USGS Crescent Valley, NV quadrangle (1:100,000 scale).
Finding the spring: From Battle Mountain travel east on Interstate 80 for 30 miles to Nevada Highway 306. Turn south onto NV 306 and go about 13 miles, passing the hamlet of Beowawe. At 13 miles or so you will see a major dirt road on your left before the highway enters the town of Crescent Valley. This dirt road is labeled McDaniel Street; turn left (east) here. Take this graded dirt road about 5 miles, bearing right at a split in the road. After 5.2 miles you will run into the largest of the hot springs up against the side of a mountain. There are two more springs farther down and across the road.

The hot springs: Set along the base of a mountain, the largest of the Crescent Valley springs is too hot to bathe in. BE CAREFUL! This large pool is a rather amazing geologic feature, however, and is worth looking at. The other two springs are across the road, a little farther down. These springs are cooler and much shallower—maybe too cool for your tastes if you enjoy a hot bath. The smaller springs do have a substantial amount of mud in them, unlike some of the more sandy-bottomed springs described in this book. The springs are in a nice location, though, and offer an excellent view of Crescent Valley. Some of the several houses nearby appear largely abandoned. Perhaps by the time you read this there will have been additional attempts at settlement in the area.

Cortez, Tenabo, and Gold Acres: Crescent Valley is cattle country, and has been for more than a century. Its products have long served mining communities in the surrounding area. A trio of ghost towns—Cortez, Tenabo, and Gold Acres, which at one time were supplied by Crescent Valley—make a good regional side trip. Each of the towns sprung up around gold mining originally, then quickly declined like so many other Nevada boomtowns. Recently, mining has revisited the area, particularly at Gold Acres, and a few people live in and around the old townsites.

To reach Cortez, simply continue south on NV 306 south of Crescent Valley, staying on the main road as it enters the mountains. Watch for signs for this town along the road (although vandals have been known to remove or damage them sufficiently to render them unreadable). To reach Tenabo and Gold Acres, follow NV 306 south out of Crescent Valley, turning right after 6 miles. The road should also be marked with signs to Tenabo and Gold Acres, but occasionally this sign is also missing.

23

Reese River Valley Hot Spring

General description: A large hot spring emanating from a small travertine hill, flowing into a small pond. Located adjacent to an abandoned farmstead in an isolated part of northern Nevada.

Location: North-central Nevada, about 35 miles south of Battle Mountain and 53 miles north of Austin.

Primitive/developed: Primitive, except for the diversion of water to a plastic tub.

Best time of year: Fall, winter, and spring. Summers can be hot.

Restrictions: None.

Access: Most passenger cars can make the trip.

Water temperature: 130 degrees F. at source, 100 degrees F. in pond.

Nearby attractions: The historic town of Austin.

Services: None; the nearest gasoline, food, and lodging can be found in Battle Mountain, 35 miles north, or in Austin, 53 miles south.

Reese River Valley Hot Spring

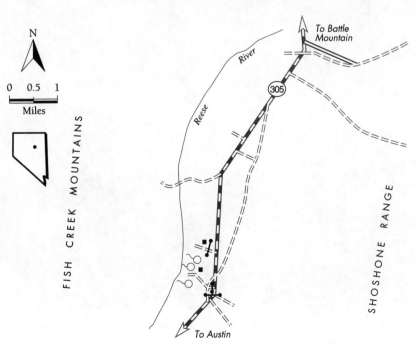

Camping: There do not appear to be any restrictions against camping at the site. The hot springs are close to the highway, however, so they may not be the most serene camping spot. There are no developed campsites in the immediate area.

Map: USGS Fish Creek Mountains, NV quadrangle (1:100,000 scale).

Finding the spring: From Battle Mountain travel south out of town on Nevada Highway 305 for about 35 miles. Keep an eye out for a small road on your right with a cattle gate. Turn right (west) onto this road, closing the cattle gate behind you. Keep right at a Y in the road. You'll reach the spring after a few hundred yards. There's a small, abandoned farmstead nearby.

The hot springs: In the dry Reese River Valley country, this hot spring is a short half-hour drive from Battle Mountain or a little more than an hour's drive from Austin. The area is dotted with abandoned farmsteads, although most of the country is still used for growing alfalfa and raising cattle. Of the several hot spring sources here, the most productive is on a small hillside composed almost entirely of travertine. Hot water emerges from a small pond at approximately 130 degrees F., and is far too hot to bathe in. Its clear water is an appealing turquoise. This water flows down a narrow, travertine-lined creek into a small pond, where it cools to about 100 degrees F. This lower pool has been used for watering cattle, but it can also provide a decent bathing opportu-

Reese River Valley Hot Spring.

nity, particularly when more water is diverted into it. Although close to the road, the spring does not appear to be heavily visited, and little trash has been left behind. Other springs in the area are much smaller (seeps) with no pools to speak of. Like so many other springs listed in this part of Nevada, the Reese River Hot Springs are located in a broad and scenic valley between two prominent ridges.

24

Leach Hot Springs

General description: Several extremely hot sources of water emerging from the ground immediately off a major graded dirt road.

Location: North-central Nevada, about 26 miles south of Winnemucca.

Primitive/developed: Primitive, except for diversion of water into a holding pond.

Best time of year: Fall, winter, or spring. Summer can be hot.

Restrictions: Private property is nearby, so be sure to obey all "no trespassing" signs.

Access: Most passenger cars can make the trip.

Water temperature: 140 degrees F. at source, varying in other pools depending upon distance from source.

Nearby attractions: Winnemucca, Jersey Valley Hot Spring, and Hyder Hot Spring.

Services: None; the nearest gasoline, food, and lodging can be found in Winnemucca, 26 miles away.

Camping: Obey all "no trespassing" signs on nearby private property. The springs are immediately off the road, so they may not be the best place to camp. Head for undeveloped space in the immediate vicinity—there's plenty of it.

Map: USGS Winnemucca, NV quadrangle (1:100,000 scale).

Finding the spring: From Winnemucca, travel south on Grass Valley Road. This paved road becomes Nevada Highway 294. Travel south for about 26 miles—the road surface turns to dirt a few miles out of town, but it is graded so most passenger cars should have no problem. Shortly before the road makes a hard left turn, look for the hot springs immediately to your left (east). The springs flow under the road in a small culvert and into a small creek. A faint dirt road follows this creek to the right (east). Take this dirt road along the creek for about 0.5 mile to where the road turns left and reaches a stock pond. There are several places along the creek where bathing is possible.

The hot springs: The hot springs on the left (east) side of the road are small and extremely hot sources of water that bubble up from the base of a small hillside. Do not attempt to bathe at these sources. Instead, follow the hot spring water to where it flows across the road and eventually coalesces into a small creek. Part of this creek has been diverted so that all the water flows into a stock pond farther downhill, and eventually to a working ranch. Although the pond is muddy and uninviting, bathing is possible in the creek at several places. Choose the spot that's right for you, provided it's not on private property. Be sure to check the water temperature before you get in.

You can reach Jersey Valley Hot Spring and Hyder Hot Spring from the same road, but it is a long drive, and far from any towns. Continue south on NV 294 beyond Leach Hot Spring, staying on the main road into Buffalo Valley and, eventually, Jersey Valley. Follow all signs to Jersey Valley and the springs (see Springs 26 and 27). Be sure you have enough gas before departing on this extended trip.

Leach Hot Springs

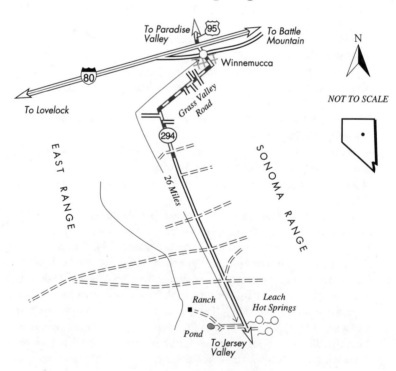

Leach Hot Springs.

25

Kyle Hot Spring

General description: A fairly large source that at one time sustained a small resort—an excellent place to bathe or visit.

Location: Northern Nevada, about 56 miles southwest of Winnemucca, and 68 miles northeast of Lovelock.

Primitive/developed: Kyle Hot Springs was once a small resort with a hot pool, steam shacks, and several outbuildings. A small cement pool has been built around the source, and water is also diverted into a few watering troughs. Lack of use means this spring is rather primitive at present.

Best time of year: Year-round.

Restrictions: None.

Access: Most passenger cars can make the trip.

Water temperature: About 110 degrees F. at the cement pool, 90 degrees F. at the watering trough.

Nearby attractions: Ghost town of Unionville.

Services: None; the nearest gasoline, food, and lodging can be found in

Winnemucca, 56 miles away. Do not count on getting supplies at hamlets such as Imlay, Mill City, and Oreana along Interstate 80.

Camping: There do not appear to be any restrictions against camping. Keep in mind, however, that there are no developed sites in the immediate vicinity. If you do camp at Kyle Hot Spring, please pack out all your trash and respect other people's privacy. Developed campgrounds may be found at Rye Patch Reservoir Recreation Area, 42 miles away along I-80.

Map: USGS Winnemucca, NV quadrangle (1:100,000 scale).

Finding the spring: From Winnemucca travel west on I-80 for 29 miles to Mill City and Nevada Highway 400. Travel south on NV 400 for 16 miles or so until you see a graded dirt road on your left. This road may or may not have a sign indicating Kyle Hot Spring. Either way, turn left here and drive 9 miles to a fork in the road. Stay left and continue up a small hill less than 0.5 mile to the hot spring.

The hot spring: Kyle Hot Spring was once a mineral bath resort offering lodging, hot baths, and steam treatments. Long abandoned, vestiges of the resort can still be seen. Across the road from the main source of water is what's left of a small adobe building. Another structure, built over several steam vents downhill from the hot spring, at one time provided steam baths. The spring has obviously been used by countless generations.

Following the abandonment of the resort, the baths fell into disrepair. A local cattleman from Lovelock cemented in the hot spring to provide bathing opportunities and subsequently fenced in the tub to keep cows out. Although this cement tub is largely stagnant now, spring water is diverted to a trough a few yards downhill, where the water is pleasantly warm and much cleaner. The view from the trough is beautiful. The hot spring is better known than most in this portion of Nevada, so seclusion is not guaranteed. Partygoers continue to trash the area, leaving garbage and vandalizing the remains of the structures. Please respect this area before someone feels the need to bulldoze the spring and its surroundings.

Unionville: Once the county seat for Humboldt, Unionville was a thriving town with several hundred people, a large bank, and a newspaper. The town was established following the discovery of silver in the nearby mountains in 1861 by two Frenchmen who maintained a trading post on the emigrant trail along the Humboldt River.

Following a rush to the region, two prospectors, Hugo Pfersdorff and J. C. Hannan, found abundant silver in Buena Vista Canyon. Unionville grew rapidly, as did its sister town Star City in Buena Vista Canyon. Unionville's greatest production came in the years between 1863 and 1870, with a population reaching 1,500 at one point. Intensive mining activity led directly to the

Kyle Hot Spring

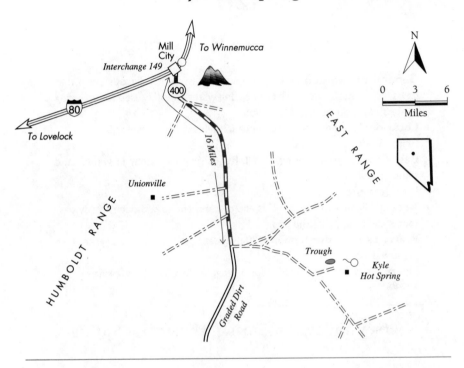

settlement of Paradise Valley in 1864, where locals grew crops and raised cattle to support the many people at Unionville. The people of Unionville nearly panicked during the Paiute War of 1865, and their newspaper, *The Humboldt Register,* discussed the events with great concern.

By 1870, the mines at Unionville had declined considerably in production. With the completion of the Central Pacific Railroad along the Humboldt, Winnemucca emerged as the region's commercial center. It is hard to imagine a bustling community at Unionville, one of the largest towns in Nevada, existing in this now empty portion of the state.

Much remains of the old town of Unionville, including several houses and portions of the old bank building. Like many Nevada ghost towns, Unionville is still occupied by a few hardy souls. To reach the townsite, travel south on NV 400. North of the turnoff for Kyle Hot Spring, you will see a sign for Unionville on the right. Take this well-maintained dirt road right (west) toward the mountains. The road leads directly to the townsite, located in a canyon.

26

Jersey Valley Hot Spring

General description: A large pool with a strong, sulfurous smell that flows into a smaller pool. The hot spring water runoff is used for watering cattle and produces lush vegetation.

Location: Northern Nevada, about 62 miles east of Lovelock.

Primitive/developed: Primitive.

Best time of year: Spring or fall. Roads may be muddy in winter, and summer can be hot.

Restrictions: None.

Access: High-clearance vehicles are recommended, although sturdy passenger cars can make the trip.

Water temperature: About 130 degrees F. at source; 110 degrees F. in the lower pool.

Nearby attractions: Hyder Hot Spring, Dixie Valley Hot Spring.

Jersey Valley Hot Spring, Hyder Hot Spring

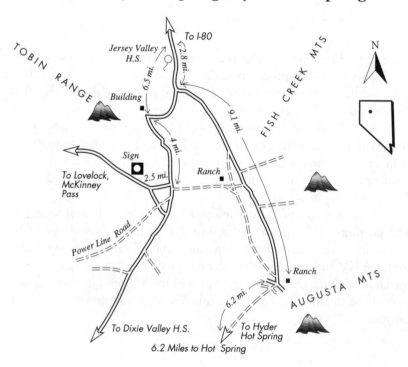

Services: None; the nearest gasoline, food, and lodging can be found in Lovelock, 62 miles away. Plan ahead.

Camping: There do not appear to be restrictions against camping at this spring, but there are no developed campsites closer than those at Rye Patch Reservoir, 85 miles away along Interstate 80.

Map: USGS Fish Creek Mountains, NV quadrangle (1:100,000 scale).

Finding the spring: From Lovelock, travel north on I-80 for 5.3 miles to Coal Canyon Road, Exit 112. Turn right (east) and go 13 miles on this paved road until you reach a sign for Dixie Valley. Turn left here and travel another 31 miles to a Y in the road with another sign to Dixie Valley. Stay right at this intersection. Follow this road another 8 miles to second Y intersection, this one with several small wooden road markers. Stay left at this intersection, following the sign to Jersey Valley. Go another 2.5 miles to a T intersection, turning left along a power line road. Stay on this main road for about 10.5 miles to the hot spring, immediately off the road to the left.

The hot spring: In a dry cattle-ranching valley, Jersey Valley Hot Spring is a long drive on a dirt road from any town. But the hot spring is worth the trip, and is near several other springs. Green vegetation and a sulfurous smell will give away the spring's location.

The source itself is an ominous pit with steaming water and muddy bottom and sides. DO NOT BATHE HERE! This hot spring water flows downhill along a small creek and is diverted into a small pool, about 2 by 4 feet and 3 feet deep. The water in this smaller pool is about 110 degrees F. Because the

Jersey Valley Hot Spring.

77

flow of the main hot spring varies, sometimes this smaller pool is shallow, stagnant, and unappealing. It can make a nice bath at times, though.

This is cattle-grazing country, and one of the area's large ranches is a few miles down the road. Although evidence of cattle is present at the hot springs, they have not completely trampled the small pool and surrounding vegetation. Be sure to watch for cattle on the road on your way to this spring, however, since there are likely to be many in the immediate vicinity.

27

Hyder Hot Spring

(See map on page 76.)

General description: A large, colorful hot spring source on an isolated hillside. Water from a smaller hot spring is trapped in a small, shallow pool that is bathable.

Location: Northern Nevada, about 62 miles from Lovelock.

Primitive/developed: Primitive.

Best time of year: Spring or fall. Roads can be muddy in winter, and summer can be hot.

Restrictions: None.

Access: High-clearance vehicles are recommended, although many sturdy passenger cars (vans, etc.) can make the trip. During wet periods, you may need four-wheel drive.

Water temperature: 130 degrees F. at source, 95 degrees F. in shallow pool.

Nearby attractions: Jersey Valley Hot Spring, Dixie Valley Hot Spring.

Services: None; the nearest gasoline, food, and lodging can be found in Lovelock, 65 miles away on mostly dirt roads. Plan ahead when traveling to this hot spring.

Camping: No restrictions against camping at the hot spring. Although the site is undeveloped, it makes an excellent place to spend the night.

Map: USGS Fish Creek Mountains, NV quadrangle (1:100,000 scale).

Finding the spring: From Jersey Valley Hot Spring (see Spring 26), go back (south) on the main road. Stay on this road for 2.8 miles until you intersect another smaller road on your left. Take this road and travel about 9.1 miles to a T intersection. Turn right here (on your left you will see a large ranch) and look for the first road on your left after about 0.2 mile. Take this lesser dirt road, keeping to the main track, for 6.2 miles or so until the road reaches a small hill/mound. On the other side of this mound,

Hyder Hot Spring.

near the top, is where the main hot spring source is located. The smaller source and small bathing pool are around the side of the hill, near the base.

The hot spring: Hyder Hot Spring rests on a small hill in an isolated portion of northern Nevada. The source itself is a large brown mound formed by mineral precipitate from the hot spring and algae living off the hot water. The hot spring water flows downhill to nurture green grasses and reeds, frequently visited by local cattle. Another smaller and less obvious source of hot water is farther downhill where water bubbles up out of the ground, eventually flowing into a small, dammed pool. This pool presents the only bathing opportunity at Hyder Hot Spring, and is about 3 by 5 feet and 1 foot deep, at about 95 degrees F.

The hill on which Hyder Hot Spring rests presents a nice vantage point on a clear day, from which most of Jersey Valley and Dixie Valley can be seen. Another hot spring, Seven Devils, lies in the same valley but on private property. The spring is conspicuous because of its site on a small hill marked by a single tree, barbed-wire fences, and "no trespassing" signs. Perhaps one day the public will be able to enjoy Seven Devils Hot Spring but, until then, respect the landowner's wishes.

28

Dixie Valley Hot Springs

General description: Numerous difficult-to-spot seeps in an isolated portion of northern Nevada. Despite few well-defined bathing spots, ample places allow for the creation of small pools with appropriate temperatures.
Location: Northern Nevada, about 75 miles northeast of Fallon.
Primitive/developed: Primitive.
Best time of year: Fall, winter, or spring. Summers can be hot.
Restrictions: Many springs are on the other side of a barbed-wire fence, although at the time of publication there were no posted "no trespassing" signs.
Access: Most passenger cars can make the trip.
Water temperature: Varies—130 degrees F. at most sources, decreasing as water flows away from the source.
Nearby attractions: Ghost town site of Wonder, remains of a Pony Express station, Sand Hill.

Dixie Valley Hot Springs.

Dixie Valley Hot Springs

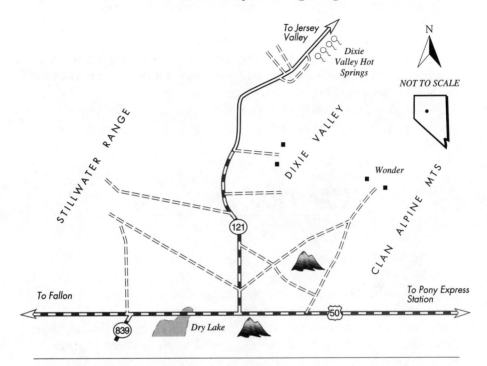

Services: None; the nearest gasoline, food, and lodging can be found in Fallon, 75 miles away. There are no services in Dixie Valley.

Camping: This is not the best camping spot, since the springs are all immediately off the road and most are on the far side of a barbed-wire fence. There is plenty of undeveloped space in the immediate vicinity, however.

Map: USGS Carson Sink, NV quadrangle (1:100,000 scale).

Finding the spring: From Fallon travel east on U.S. Highway 50 for 38 miles. Turn left (north) onto Nevada Highway 121 and take it about 37.5 miles to the hot springs. This paved road will turn into a graded dirt road. Keep an eye out for darker vegetation off to your right. Also watch for another dirt road on the right; the series of hot seeps begins immediately after this road meets the main graded road. Various hot springs are found alongside the road for the next 0.25 mile.

The hot springs: Consisting of several separate clusters of springs, the Dixie Valley Hot Springs present a marked contrast to this desert valley. The series of seeps extends about 0.25 mile. Although the springs vary in temperature, they are all extremely hot at their sources (130 to 150 degrees F.). Do not bathe anywhere near the sources! Almost all the springs run into small creeks that flow as far as a few hundred yards. The water cools as it flows from the source, there are bathing opportunities here, although it would mean clearing a substantial amount of brush. If you are going to attempt to bathe in water from these springs, be sure to let any diverted water cool sufficiently, and check the temperature before getting in.

Few people pass through this part of Nevada, which offers several other hot springs to explore on your own.

CENTRAL NEVADA

Anchored in the west by the state capitol at Carson City, Central Nevada provides a wealth of tourist activities. Even less populated than the northern parts of the state, the area offers ample outdoor recreation opportunities. Like other areas of Nevada, Central Nevada possesses thousands of acres of public land. The region also contains several large mining districts, particularly in its eastern half. Several high mountain ranges break up the country. Many of the higher reaches of these ranges are controlled by Toiyabe National Forest, with abundant hiking trails, campgrounds, and places of historical and archaeological interest.

GARDNERVILLE, MINDEN, AND THE CARSON VALLEY

Immediately south of Reno and Carson City are the beautiful communities of Minden and Gardnerville. These small, primarily ranching towns rest at the base of the majestic Sierra Nevada, and are well watered from snowmelt. The area contains the oldest settlement in Nevada, the community of Genoa, established by Mormon pioneers in the 1850s. Minden and Gardnerville are also situated at the confluence of several major roads, taking you to a myriad of points beyond. Although there are several hot springs resorts in the immediate vicinity, the only truly unharnessed hot spring is included here.

29

SARATOGA HOT SPRING

General description: A high-temperature hot spring flowing out of a small hill below a paved road. The water flows down a creek and eventually into two bathable pools. Near Carson City, this well-known spring is a pleasant spot that, if visited at the right time, can feel secluded.

Location: West-central Nevada, about 10 miles south of Carson City.

Primitive/developed: Primitive, except for the damming of creek flow into two pools.

Best time of year: Year-round.

Restrictions: The spring is almost completely surrounded by private property. At times, the area has been closed due to problems related to late-night partying, etc.

Access: Paved road to the source. The short drive to the bathable pools is a little sandy in places, but most passenger cars with decent clearance should be fine. The pools are only a few hundred yards from the road, if you prefer to walk.

Water temperature: 120 degrees F. at source, varying from 95 to 110 degrees F. in the pools.

Nearby attractions: Lake Tahoe, Virginia City.

Services: None; the nearest gasoline, food, and lodging can be found in Carson City, 10 miles away. This is not an isolated area, so don't worry too much about finding food, gas, or supplies.

Camping: Although this would make a nice overnight spot, local convention says camping is not allowed at the pools or the hot spring source. Seek out any of several developed campgrounds in the area.

Map: USGS Carson City, NV quadrangle (1:100,000 scale).

Finding the spring: From Carson City, travel south on U.S. Highway 395 about 6 miles to Stephanie Way, and turn left. Follow Stephanie Way for about 2 miles to Vicky Lane, and turn left again. Follow Vicky Lane 1.1 miles or so until you see a small, concrete structure downhill on the left. The hot spring emerges here, on the left side of the road, immediately after the pavement ends. If you wish to drive on to the pools, turn left immediately before the pavement ends on a dirt road, following it for less than 0.5 mile to the first pool. Be forewarned—this second road is sandy in places.

The hot spring: Also known as Mission Hot Springs, Saratoga is adjacent

Saratoga Hot Spring

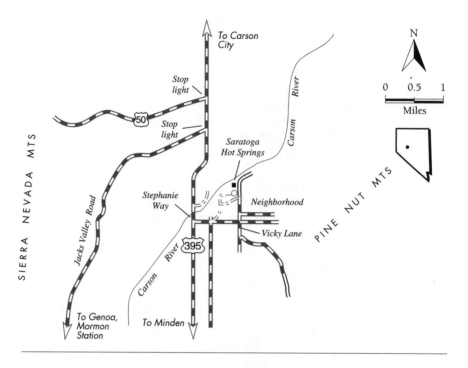

to a large and growing neighborhood in the valley between Carson City and Minden/Gardnerville. The water flowing from the source on the other side of the road is too hot for bathing until it reaches the first pool. At the pools, the water ranges in temperature, but makes for a nice soak. The water is generally clear, and the pools are 2 to 3 feet deep with sandy bottoms. Several cottonwoods shade the area, a pleasant spot except when partygoers leave trash here. The spring has seen problems in the past, including fights and general drunkenness. Don't expect to get the area to yourself, unless you arrive on a weekday in fall or spring.

Hot spring resorts in the area: The two major, developed hot springs in the area are Walleys Hot Spring Resort and Carson Hot Springs. Walleys Hot Spring Resort, (702) 782-8155, offers several outdoor and indoor hot pools, and rooms for overnight stays. To reach it, travel south on US 395 from Carson City. Immediately past the turnoff for U.S. Highway 50 to Lake Tahoe is a traffic signal at Jack's Valley Road. Turn right (west) here, and drive a little more than 5 miles to the resort on your left (east). If you continue on Jack's Valley

Road you will reach the small, quaint town of Genoa, with Mormon Station, a historic site run by the State of Nevada. Carson Hot Springs, (702) 882-9863, in Carson City itself, offers private indoor hot springs and an outdoor public pool. To reach Carson Hot Springs, travel north through Carson City and turn east (right) on Hot Springs Road at the north end of town, continuing about 1 mile farther to the facility.

Mormon Station: Established in 1850 as a trading post along the emigrant trail to California, the small cabin at present-day Genoa was at that time within Utah Territory. The territory created under the Compromise of 1850 had given the Mormon settlement at Salt Lake City, led by Brigham Young, control over an area covering present-day Utah, most of Nevada, and portions of Colorado. As Mormons sought to spread their settlements beyond Salt Lake City, members of the church were sent to distant lands, including the eastern slope of the Sierra Nevada. Although there was a Mormon community at Genoa, the majority of the settlers here were non-Mormon "Gentiles" who desired a government of their own. Seeing that the territorial government in Salt Lake City treated the Carson Valley settlement with disinterest, the settlers eventually wrote their own constitution, proposing that a new territory be carved out

Saratoga Hot Spring.

of portions of the state of California and the territory of Utah. Many of these early meetings were held in this original trading post. Despite changing ownership, the post remains (with many renovations) to the present day.

As a result of this constitutional convention, however, Mormon leadership in Salt Lake City was aroused sufficiently to dispatch a large group of settlers to the Carson Valley in 1855. Because of friction between the federal government and the Mormon territory of Utah, Brigham Young recalled all outlying settlers back to Salt Lake City in 1857, fearing the approach of war. This Mormon exodus left the Gentiles in firm control of Carson Valley once again.

Despite several political meetings by the settlers to establish some form of local government, little was accomplished. The discovery of gold, and later silver, in mountains to the north and east did not improve this political inactivity. The boom at the Comstock Lode established Virginia City, which would be the largest town in Nevada for the next fifty years. The mines brought settlers into the mountains, shifting focus away from the Carson Valley. At the onset of the Civil War, the settlements in western Utah were finally organized as a distinct territory—Nevada—in 1861.

FALLON AND THE CARSON SINK

Although there is only one hot spring in the Fallon area, the region is worth visiting—especially if you enjoy desert solitude and archaeology. At the edge of the Carson Sink where the Carson River disappears into the desert, Fallon has long been an agricultural center. Irrigated by water from manmade Lake Lahonton, the town grew up from one of the first reclamation projects in the country. The presence of the Fallon Naval Air Station, and with it the transfer of the Navy's TOPGUN fighter weapons training program, the town has benefited from a variety of economic pursuits. East of Fallon stretches U.S. Highway 50, the path of the old Pony Express, now called the "Loneliest Road in America."

Two spectacular archaeological sites also exist within close range of Fallon. Grimes Point, a self-guided trail along the edges of a prehistoric lake, contains boulders and rocks replete with petroglyphs. The site is about 12 miles east of Fallon on US 50. Further information can be obtained from the Bureau of Land Management at (702) 885-6000. Hidden Cave, another spectacular archaeological site in the area, allows visitors to see a prehistoric storage site. It can be accessed by guided tour. For information call (702) 423-3677.

30

Lee Hot Spring

General description: A largely dry hot spring in Central Nevada that at one time produced enough water for a decent bath. The geologic aspect of the spring and local scenery make up for the limited bathable pools.
Location: Central Nevada, about 19 miles south of Fallon.
Primitive/developed: Primitive, except for diversion of water into a cattle-watering area.
Best time of year: Winter, spring, or fall. Summer can be too hot.
Restrictions: None.
Access: Most passenger cars can make the trip.
Water temperature: 120 degrees F. at source. When there was more water, it cooled to about 100 degrees F. in a small pool near the source.

Lee Hot Spring

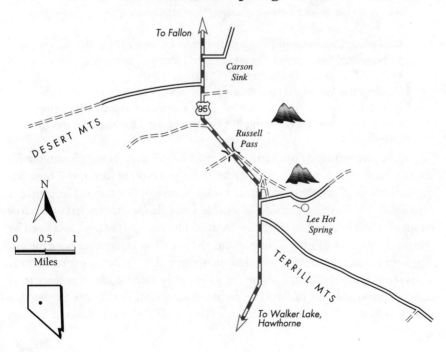

Lee Hot Spring.

Nearby attractions: Grimes Point Archaeological Site, Hidden Cave.
Services: None; the nearest gasoline, food, and lodging can be found in Fallon, 19 miles away.
Camping: Undeveloped camping appears to be permitted in the vicinity of the spring. The surrounding area also has plenty of public land.
Map: USGS Fallon, NV quadrangle (1:100,000 scale).
Finding the spring: From Fallon travel south out of town on U.S. Highway 95 for about 18 miles. Turn left onto a dirt road shortly after going over Russell Pass. Travel on this dirt road for about 0.8 mile to the spring.

The hot spring: At one time this hot spring produced enough water to fill a small pool, which made a nice bath. More recently, however, the flow has decreased, and all that can be seen is a small source of hot water. The source is on a small hill on the other side of a cattle fence. If the air temperature is low enough, it will have steam emerging from it. The flow might have increased by the time you read this book, but if not, the source is interesting nonetheless. The setting for the spring is picturesque, though dry. Evidence for prehistoric inhabitants is also present. This spring is definitely worth a stop if you are traveling in the vicinity of Fallon. The archaeological sites in the area are worth a visit, and Walker Lake, about 35 miles south on US 95, offers excellent fishing, boating, and general sightseeing.

MONITOR VALLEY AND TOIYABE NATIONAL FOREST

The mountains and valleys east of Austin are some of the most scenic parts of central Nevada, offering much of interest. Austin itself is a living ghost town, surviving from its glory days of the early 1860s. Several other, less lived-in ghost towns dot the landscape, including Belmont, Berlin, and Ione. The Toiyabe Range south of Austin contains peaks as high as 11,773 feet and is bordered on the east and west by other ranges almost as high. Although roads into these mountains are few, and generally poor, visitors have other ways to escape the heat of the valleys below. Between the Toiyabe and Monitor ranges lies the well-watered Monitor Valley, home to several hot springs. The Monitor Valley is cattle-ranching country with ghost towns (such as Belmont), abundant wildlife, and beautiful scenery. Be aware that most springs in this region are well off the beaten track and require preparation. If you plan to travel into the high country, be prepared for colder (and possibly wetter) conditions than those in the valleys. As usual, stay away from dirt roads when they're wet, and be wary of changing weather patterns.

31

Spencer Hot Springs

General description: A series of hot springs on the site of an old resort in an isolated part of central Nevada. There are both natural hot spring pools and a watering trough that has hot spring water diverted into it. Bathing opportunities are some of the best in the area. These are relatively well-known hot springs, but definitely worth a visit.
Location: Central Nevada, about 20 miles southeast of Austin.
Primitive/developed: Primitive, except for the diversion of hot spring water into a tub.
Best time of year: Fall, spring, or summer. Roads can be quite muddy in wet winter months.
Restrictions: None.
Access: Most passenger cars can make the trip, but you will need four-wheel drive in extremely wet weather.
Water temperature: Varying depending on the pond—110 degrees F. in one, 105 degrees F. in the others. The temperature also varies in the

Spencer Hot Springs

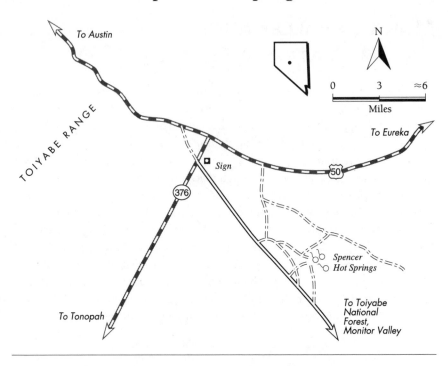

natural pond depending upon where in the tub you sit.

Nearby attractions: Historic town of Austin, Toiyabe National Forest.

Services: None; the nearest gasoline, food, and lodging can be found in Austin, 20 miles away.

Camping: There is plenty of camping space near the hot springs. You may have to share the area with others, however. Be sure to camp away from the springs themselves and respect other people's privacy. There are also plenty of campsites in Toiyabe National Forest to the east. These campsites are at higher elevations and will be substantially cooler, with snow in winter.

Map: USGS Summit Mountains, NV quadrangle (1:100,000 scale).

Finding the spring: From Austin, travel east on U.S. Highway 50 for 12 miles. Turn right (south) onto Nevada Highway 376 and go about 100 yards. Turn left (east) on a large, graded dirt road with Forest Service signs indicating Toquime Cave. Travel on this graded dirt road for 5.5 miles or so to a dirt road on the left. Turn left. Go approximately 3 miles, bearing right at a Y in the road for another 1.6 miles to the springs.

The hot springs: Spencer Hot Springs basically consists of three hot springs. The lower hot spring is adjacent to an abandoned swimming pool that has

Spencer Hot Springs.

since been bulldozed. The spring is now diverted through a metal pipe to a round watering trough. This trough makes an excellent bath, since the water is kept relatively clean by the constant flow of water. The temperature is also kept relatively constant at 105 degrees F. The other two springs are up the hill, and consist of natural pools formed by hot spring water. One of the springs is about 5 by 7 feet, and about 3 feet deep. This spring is also excellent for bathing. The temperature hovers around 110 degrees F., and the water is just deep enough to provide a good soak. A small wooden deck has been built adjacent to the pool. The other upper spring is less desirable, since it is shallower and much cooler. I have yet to see anyone bathe in this one. All three of the springs are far enough away from each other to provide privacy and a sense of solitude.

Austin: The third mineral-rich region in Nevada, discovered after the Comstock, Austin (also known as the Reese River District) became one of the most celebrated. Lying along the old Pony Express route, it boomed after a former express rider discovered silver in Pony Canyon in 1862. News of the discovery spread quickly, and people flocked to the area to get rich. Soon afterward the County of Lander was created, and the growing hamlet of Austin was selected as its seat in 1863. Inhabitants of the neighboring communities of Houston and Jacob's Well relocated to Austin soon thereafter.

During a lull in activity at the Virginia City mines, and with increased attention from the California press, Austin's population swelled. Because its mineral discovery was overhyped, capital from all over the country streamed into town. The new residents constructed elaborate stone, brick, and wood buildings, including schools, churches, hotels, and saloons along with several expensive mills to process the ore they believed they'd find.

Although its mines' production was relatively low, Austin did serve as a base of operation from which prospectors discovered countless other strikes. These strikes, in turn, brought about the creation of new towns and, in some cases, whole new counties—Nye, White Pine, and Eureka. The town today is a shadow of its former lively self, but many of Austin's original buildings still stand. The more transient buildings are decaying rapidly and may not survive many more years of neglect. Some of the more substantial stone buildings are still in fine shape.

32

Monitor Valley Hot Springs

(See map on page 94.)

General description: Several hot springs in an isolated valley in central Nevada. The hot spring with the largest discharge is piped into a circular watering trough, providing a nice bath. The view from the spring is fantastic.
Location: Central Nevada, about 45 miles southeast of Austin and 86 miles northeast of Tonopah.
Primitive/developed: Primitive, except for the diversion of the hot spring water into a watering trough.
Best time of year: Year-round.
Restrictions: None.
Access: Most passenger cars can make the trip. The last few miles are on a less-developed road, but sturdy cars with sufficient clearance should be able to reach the springs.
Water temperature: 130 degrees F. at source, 105 degrees F. in tub.
Nearby attractions: Ghost town of Belmont, Toiyabe National Forest.
Services: None; the nearest gasoline, food, and lodging can be found in Austin, 45 miles away, or in Tonopah, 86 miles away. There are no services in Belmont.
Camping: There do not appear to be any restrictions against undeveloped camping at this spot. There are several campgrounds in the Toiyabe National Forest to the west, although these are also undeveloped sites.
Map: USGS Summit Mountains, NV quadrangle (1:100,000 scale).

Monitor Valley Hot Springs.

Finding the spring: From Austin, travel east on U.S. Highway 50 for 12 miles. Turn right (south) onto Nevada Highway 376 and go about 100 yards. Turn left on a large, graded dirt road with Forest Service signs indicating Toquime Cave. Travel past the turnoff to Spencer Hot Springs (Spring 31), continuing on the main graded dirt road. This Forest Service road takes you up into the mountains and Toiyabe National Forest. Take this road about 28 miles into the next valley to the east, Monitor Valley. About 28 miles from the intersection with NV 376 you will reach the Monitor Valley Road; turn right (south) here. Travel on this equally well-maintained road for 3.8 miles to a Y in the road, where you stay left. From the Y, go another 2.1 miles to Forest Road 25. Turn here and take this road across a creek and past an abandoned farmhouse. Travel another 1 mile to another dirt road on your right, which takes you directly to the spring.

The hot springs: Like many other hot springs in northern and central Nevada, the Monitor Valley Hot Springs flow into a broad valley used for grazing. Like the other springs, these are also isolated. But unlike some of the others, they are not well known. You should have no problem with privacy here.

The largest flowing spring is diverted into a circular watering trough where the water cools from 130 degrees F. at the source to about 105 degrees F. in the trough. The water in the trough is relatively uniform in temperature and stays fairly clean due to the constant inflow and outflow of water. The trough is about 6 feet across and 3 feet deep. Cattle do utilize this area, but the trough is generally clean and provides a great bath in a great location.

33

Diana's Punch Bowl

General description: An immense travertine hill with a pit in the middle, about 50 feet across, with hot spring water in the bottom. The hill is visible from miles away and truly awe-inspiring upon inspection. Although it is impossible to bathe at the main source, there are other smaller sources at the base of the hill.

Location: Central Nevada, about 50 miles southeast of Austin and 80 miles northeast of Tonopah.

Monitor Valley Hot Springs, Diana's Punch Bowl

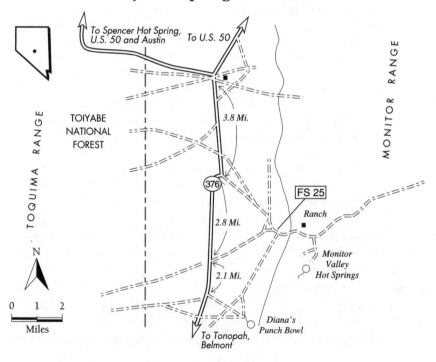

Diana's Punch Bowl.

Primitive/developed: Primitive.

Best time of year: Year-round.

Restrictions: Be extremely careful if driving up the travertine hill. Do not try it at night! Be sure to close any cattle gates.

Access: Most passenger cars can make the trip to the hill. I don't recommend driving up the travertine hill, but if you are going to do so, you may want a car with decent clearance and power.

Water temperature: 190 degrees F. at source, 110 degrees F. in the tubs at the margin of the hill.

Nearby attractions: Ghost town of Belmont, Toiyabe National Forest.

Services: None; the nearest gasoline, food, and lodging can be found in Winnemucca, 50 miles away, or in Tonopah, 80 miles away. There are no services in Belmont.

Camping: I do not recommend camping on the travertine hill. There is plenty of space for undeveloped camping at the base of the hill, where there are other hot springs. There are also campgrounds in Toiyabe National Forest, although these are also undeveloped.

Map: USGS Summit Mountains, NV quadrangle (1:100,000 scale).

Finding the spring: From Austin travel east on U.S. Highway 50 for 12 miles. Turn right (south) onto Nevada Highway 376 and go about 100 yards. Turn left on a large, graded dirt road with Forest Service signs indicating Toquime Cave. Travel on this road past the turnoff to Spencer Hot

Spring (Spring 31). Go about 28 miles into the Monitor Valley, turning right on the Monitor Valley Road. Travel on this road as if you were going to Monitor Valley Hot Springs (Spring 32), bearing right at the Y in the road after 3.8 miles. Continue past Forest Road 25, however, staying on the main road. Travel approximately 4.9 miles to a dirt road on the left (east), until you reach another intersection, where you turn left. After another 2.1 miles turn left again on a fairly well-maintained road. By this time you will see the large, white travertine hill. Go another 1.3 miles to the hill, passing through a cattle gate, which you must close behind you.

The hot springs: One of the most amazing geologic features in the state, Diana's Punch Bowl is aptly titled. In the middle of the travertine hill is a large cavern that drops almost 30 feet to a large pool of hot water below. The cavern is about 50 feet across, and its walls are completely vertical. BE EXTREMELY CAREFUL HERE! If you fall in, there is a good chance you won't be coming out in one piece. Keep a tight hold on pets and animals. I do not recommend driving onto the hill, since the spring is only a short walk from the base. This caution applies particularly at night, when you could easily drive right into the cavern.

After staring in amazement at this creation, drive to the far side of the hill where there is a small creek fed by several hot springs. This creek is about 110 degrees F. and makes a nice spot for a break or camping. The scenery is spectacular. The green valley and high mountains in the distance provide an excellent backdrop.

The founder of the town of Tonopah, J. L. Butler, knew about Diana's Punch Bowl and visited it frequently. Butler claimed that the water level in the spring fluctuated occasionally, dropping considerably. He also mentioned that gas sometimes was emitted from the spring, and claimed to have seen flames emerge from the pit on occasion.

Belmont: Perhaps one of the best ghost towns in Nevada, Belmont is worth a special trip. On the main road from Monitor Valley to Tonopah, Belmont sits on either side of a low divide separating two valleys. The mine, mill remains, and smelter are all on the Monitor Valley side, while the townsite lies to the west at the north end of Nevada Highway 376. Founded in 1865, Belmont is one of the oldest, and most genuine ghost towns in the state. The high points of the town include a cemetery with original hand-carved, wooden grave markers, a row of original storefronts, and the magnificent Belmont Courthouse, which has had substantial recent restoration and renovation work. Because of the number of people living at Belmont, and the intensive mining activity, the town served as the Nye County seat from 1876 to 1905, when it was supplanted by Tonopah.

The stately, two-story walls of the Highbridge Ore Mill still stand just south of the smelter, illustrating just how much money was invested into this location years ago. After decreasing production of Belmont's mines by the turn of the last century, and the rise of mining at Goldfield and Tonopah, Belmont was all but abandoned by 1910. It is hard to imagine the amount and type of activity that must have occurred here at one time. The Belmont saloon is still open today, holding countless relics of the Belmont of old.

To reach Belmont, continue south on the Monitor Valley Road past Diana's Punch Bowl, following signs to Belmont and Tonopah. You will soon see the large Belmont smokestack, to the west, at the base of the mountains. Follow the main road as it approaches the smokestack and goes over a hill into the town itself. This same road will take you to NV 376, which eventually becomes a paved road, and which in turn will take you to U.S. Highway 6 after 40 miles or so. Turn right (west) on US 6 and go 5 miles to reach Tonopah.

WARM SPRINGS AREA

The least populated portion of the state so far discussed, the Warm Springs area provides unanticipated contrasts. The low desert surrounding Warm Springs can seem truly desolate and empty, until one drives into magnificent Hot Creek Valley and meets towering granite walls and lush green vegetation watered by a year-round creek. The area lies just north of the immense Nellis Air Force Base, the Nevada Test Site (for nuclear weapons), and the mysterious Area 51 and Groom Lake.

The Groom Lake region is the most isolated and highly secure portion of Nellis A.F.B., and has been referred to as "Dreamland," since for years the U.S. Air Force would not acknowledge its existence. The nearby town of Rachel is known by many as the UFO-spotting capital of the country, owing to the large number of sightings reported in the area every year. Nevada Highway 375 (on which Rachel lies) was recently renamed the Extra-Terrestrial Highway. Due to the area's lack of population, traveling in this portion of Nevada requires extra preparation. There are few towns that offer any services. There are no services at Warm Springs, and Rachel, 62 miles away, meets only the most basic needs (although there is one motel). Alamo and Ash Springs are also very small, but they, too, provide basic services.

34

Warm Springs

General description: A once-active hot springs resort in an isolated part of central Nevada. Although the bathhouse is closed, visitors can still access the hot spring itself. Portions of the creek have been dammed to provide bathing opportunities.

Location: Central Nevada, about 50 miles from Tonopah.

Primitive/developed: The developed portions of this onetime resort are all closed and fenced off. There are more primitive pools along the source creek.

Best time of year: Spring, fall, or winter. Summer can be too hot.

Restrictions: Keep out of the old pool grounds and the abandoned restaurant. Avoid private property just beyond the hot spring source.

Access: Since this site is immediately off the highway, any car can make the trip. You will need a high-clearance vehicle and possibly four-wheel drive to drive the few hundred yards to the source, or you can always walk.

Water temperature: 140 degrees F. at the source, gradually cooling as it flows downhill. By the time the water reaches the old resort, it is about 105 degrees F.

Warm Springs (Source).

Nearby attractions: Hot Creek Canyon.

Services: None; the nearest gasoline, food, and lodging can be found in Tonopah, 50 miles away. At one time there was a bar and restaurant at Warm Springs, but it is now closed.

Camping: Much of the area around the spring is private property and the spring is immediately off the highway. The surrounding area offers plenty of interesting country for undeveloped camping.

Map: USGS Warm Springs, NV quadrangle (1:100,000 scale).

Finding the spring: From Tonopah, travel east on U.S. Highway 6 for 50 miles to the abandoned bar and restaurant. You will see the closed pool. If you go around to the back, you will see the diverted creek of water. To find the source, follow the small road leading up the travertine hill behind the resort site. After 200 yards or so, this road climbs to the top of the hill. Don't try this with a regular passenger car—park and walk the last 50 to 100 yards. The spring's cooler pools are adjacent to the closed restaurant and bar, under a few small trees.

The hot springs: Also known as Nanny Goat Hot Spring, Warm Springs was quite a resort at one time, boasting a substantial pool and bathhouse. A restaurant and gas station were also open here at one time, but are now closed. The only contact with the civilized world here is a pay phone.

Warm Springs

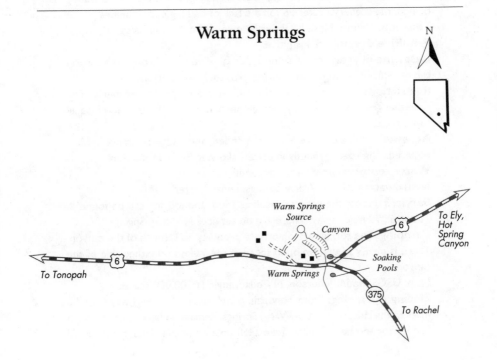

Atop a large travertine hill, water emerges from the ground here crystal-clear and extremely hot. The travertine is strikingly white, in direct contrast to the more subdued colors of the surrounding desert. Apparently the hot spring lies on a major geological fault, with several recently reported earthquakes attributed to it. Do not bathe at the source. Instead, return to the abandoned resort and look for a few small pools in the creek on the east side of the restaurant. You can also follow the water on the other side of the highway, where it is cooler and the pools are smaller.

Although this is an isolated part of the state, do not expect to have the area to yourself. Often someone is camped in an RV adjacent to the dammed-up pools, and a surprisingly large number of people pass through this region, usually stopping at Warm Springs.

35

Hot Creek Canyon

General description: A spectacular canyon in an extremely isolated portion of central Nevada. Although most hot springs in the area are privately owned, the scenery makes up for the lack of bathing opportunities.
Location: Central Nevada, about 50 miles from Winnemucca.
Primitive/developed: Primitive.
Best time of year: Spring, summer, or fall. The road through the canyon can be difficult or impassable during extremely wet periods.
Restrictions: The hot springs themselves are on private property. The road that goes past them is generally open, however. Be sure to close all cattle gates.
Access: Four-wheel drive is recommended, and a high-clearance vehicle required. The road is muddy in places, allowing for little traction.
Water temperature: Varies depending on spring.
Nearby attractions: Warm Springs, Lunar Crater.
Services: None; the nearest gasoline, food, and lodging can be found in Tonopah, 90 miles away. There are no services in Warm Springs.
Camping: The springs are on private property, as is much of the canyon. There is plenty of undeveloped space in the valleys on either side of the canyon.
Map: USGS Mount Jefferson, NV quadrangle (1:100,000 scale).
Finding the spring: From Tonopah, travel east on U.S. Highway 6 for 50 miles to the closed resort of Warm Springs. Remain on US 6, east of Warm Springs, for another 25 miles. Take a left on a well-maintained, graded road

about 2 miles before Sandy Summit; if you reach the summit, you have gone too far. Follow this graded dirt road west across the wide valley toward the mountains. After 8 miles or so you will approach the fair-sized Hot Creek Ranch. Continue on the main road toward the ranch, then take a smaller road on the right after you cross a small creek. This road passes through ranch property, but is generally open to through traffic. Follow it into the canyon where, after less than 0.5 mile from the ranch itself, you will see dark green grass and water on your right. This is the first of the hot springs that gives the canyon its name.

If you have an appropriate vehicle you can continue on this road through the length of the entire canyon, exiting into the adjacent Fish Lake Valley. If you turn left (south) when reaching this valley, you will eventually reach US 6 again, west of Warm Springs.

The hot springs: Immediately beyond the ranch, the first springs you'll see produce a large amount of water, feeding a lush, marshy area. A fence and "no trespassing" sign are between the road and the springs—respect and obey these property markers. As you pass these first springs you enter Hot Springs Canyon, which becomes narrower as you head west. The scenery grows more

Hot Creek Canyon

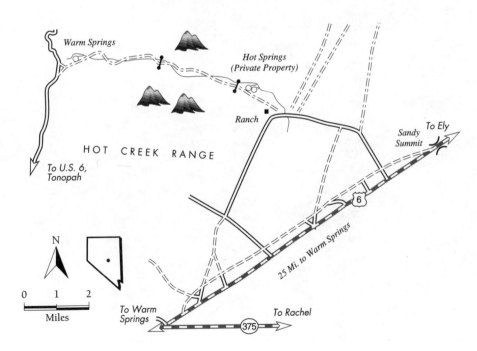

and more spectacular. The sheer canyon walls and green foliage are a far cry from the desert valleys on either side. Driving along US 6 you would never know this canyon existed.

You will pass through several cattle gates (which you must close behind you). In places the road will become muddy. There are several private homes in this isolated canyon; do not disturb them. About halfway through the valley you will reach the remains of an old ranch and home, on the north side. The ranch is known locally as the Old Dugan Place, and it is in good shape owing largely to its isolated location. There are a few cold springs in the vicinity of this ranch, plus one small warm spring that averages 90 degrees F. The spring was dug up to increase its flow for irrigation and stock watering. Personnel from the Nuclear Test Site within Nellis A.F.B. also utilized this canyon for unspecified reasons during the 1960s or 1970s. Some type of testing occurred, although details have not been made public.

About 8 miles from the ranch, the canyon begins to open up. There are several springs on either side of the road. The last in the series of springs is a warm one, with temperatures averaging 95 degrees F. Although the spring is little more than a trickle, it does makes an interesting stop. Once you get into the Fish Lake Valley on the far side of the canyon, you can turn left (south) to reach US 6 again. This road intersects with the highway in about 28 miles, placing you west of Warm Springs. To get back to Tonopah turn right on US 6.

36

Ash Springs

General description: A series of natural hot spring ponds shaded by several large trees in a picnic spot. Ash Spring is an ideal place for a soak, if you happen to be in this isolated part of the state.

Location: South-central Nevada, about 97 miles from Las Vegas.

Primitive/developed: Primitive, with an adjacent campground.

Best time of year: Fall, spring, or winter. Summers can be hot.

Restrictions: There is a private resort adjacent to the springs. Do not trespass.

Access: Most passenger cars can make the trip.

Water temperature: 110 degrees F. at the source, cooling to 95 degrees F. as it flows into small pools downstream. Another spring measures about 100 degrees F., over which a small concrete pool has been constructed.

Nearby attractions: White River Petroglyphs site, town of Rachel.

Services: Limited services can be found at the Ash Springs Resort, including gasoline, groceries, and a restaurant. For more extensive services, you must go all the way to Las Vegas.

Camping: There is no camping permitted at the springs themselves, though there are developed sites across the highway at the resort. There is plenty of BLM land for undeveloped camping in the surrounding countryside.

Map: Nevada State Highway map.

Finding the springs: From Las Vegas, travel east on Interstate 15 for 22 miles to Nevada Highway 93. Go north on NV 93 for 81 miles to the small hamlet of Alamo. Continue north on NV 93 for about 5 miles to the Ash Springs resort. Continue past the resort and immediately turn right onto a dirt road. Drive the short distance (100 yards) to the picnic area near the springs.

The hot springs: A pleasant set of hot springs, Ash Springs provide a welcome oasis in the isolated desert. Although there are several springs in the area, their outflow makes a small creek with several small pools. These pools are ideal for bathing, with relatively sandy bottoms and varied sizes and depths—always big enough to soak in. Although this is an isolated part of the state, the springs are relatively well known, easily accessible, and rather visible. Keep this in mind when bathing.

The resort on the other side of the road has many supplies and camping spaces. It may be your only choice for staying the night at Ash Springs, since there is no camping permitted at the springs themselves and there are no hotels in the immediate area.

Ash Springs

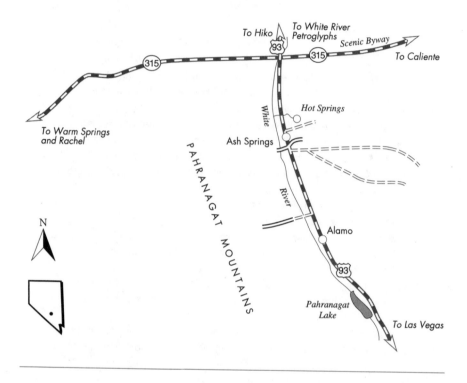

To Hiko
To White River
Petroglyphs
Scenic Byway
To Caliente
93
315
315
To Warm Springs
and Rachel
Hot Springs
White
Ash Springs
River
PAHRANAGAT MOUNTAINS
N
Alamo
93
Pahranagat
Lake
To Las Vegas

TONOPAH AND GOLDFIELD REGION

Following the demise of the great Comstock Lode in northern Nevada, a second mining boom occurred in the Goldfield–Tonopah region. As with so many mining towns in Nevada, Goldfield grew rapidly once the discovery of its rich ores became widely known. Beginning in 1900, the Goldfield area mines yielded silver in abundance. For the next twenty years, Goldfield and Tonopah would be the political, economic, and social centers of Nevada.

A poor, part-time miner by the name of John Butler prospected many portions of Nevada until, in 1900, he came across the rich outcrop upon which Tonopah would be founded. The ore discovered by Butler required the investment of outside capital, however. The first to participate was a lawyer named Tasker Oddie. With the help of an assayer and several miners, the partners were able to obtain two tons of ore, for which they received $500. The issuance of this check brought about substantial publicity, and a rush to southern Nevada.

Grubstakers hired by Butler and his associates discovered ore about 30 miles south of Tonopah in 1904. This rich discovery led to the creation of the Goldfield Mining District.

Since the land in which Tonopah and Goldfield were located was inhospitable, the founders initially had a difficult time acquiring financial backing. The region was devoid of wood, lacked water, and was far from any settlements or transportation links. Eventually backing came, largely from eastern interests, and mines began to be seriously exploited. Railroads were soon built, large mills constructed, and water companies formed. More bank money arrived, along with thousands of people. Power was brought from miles away, and the Tonopah developers experimented with more sophisticated techniques and put them to practical use in the mills. Tonopah and Goldfield were connected to major markets via several small rail lines to the Carson & Colorado Railroad in 1904. By 1905, the lines were made standard gauge and consolidated under the Tonopah & Goldfield Railroad. Soon thereafter two men, George Nixon and George Wingfield, were able to gain almost complete control over the booming towns and, to a large extent, the whole state.

It was not until 1913 that Tonopah and Goldfield saw another new advance—the automobile. Because of the mining towns' isolated locations, and because roads in and out were poor, the automobile did not become a major source of transportation until well after the towns' decline. By the late 1910s the boom days were over, and population dropped after 1920. Many other towns, including Bullfrog and Rhyolite, sprung up in the nearby deserts, but all of them withered away as fast as they developed. Although a few people still live in Goldfield today, the largest town in the area is Tonopah, which subsists on mining, tourism, and the military.

37

Alkali Hot Springs

General description: Two hot springs in a small oasis in the middle of dry central Nevada. One of the springs is diverted into a makeshift tub, making a nice bath.

Location: West-central Nevada, about 11 miles west of Goldfield and 27 miles southwest of Tonopah.

Primitive/developed: Primitive, except for the diversion of water into the tub.

Best time of year: Fall, winter, or spring. Summer can be hot.

Restrictions: There are "no trespassing" signs in the area. Heed them.

Access: Most passenger cars can make the trip to the springs, which are immediately off a paved highway.

Water temperature: About 120 degrees F. at source, 110 degrees F. in tub.

Nearby attractions: The historic mining town of Goldfield.

Services: None; gasoline, food, and lodging can be found in Tonopah, 27 miles away, and Goldfield, 11 miles away. There are few services in Goldfield, which is a ghost of its originally boisterous self.

Camping: This is not the most ideal place to camp, since the springs are immediately off the road. There are also many "no trespassing" signs in the vicinity. Look for undeveloped camping space in the surrounding area.

Map: USGS Goldfield, NV quadrangle (1:100,000 scale).

Finding the springs: From Tonopah, travel south on U.S. Highway 95 for 21 miles, then turn right (west) on the road to Silverpeak and Alkali. From Goldfield, travel north on U.S. Highway 95 for 4 miles, turning left on the Silverpeak road. Take this paved road about 6.8 miles. After rounding a curve you will see the remains of a building on your left, which lies adjacent to the hot springs. Pull off the road in the broad, flat area and seek out the hot springs on the side of the hill.

The hot springs: Hot water emerges from the side of a small hill in a desert area. A few trees and an empty pool mark what was at one time a hot springs resort. The hot water is trapped in two separate pools of varying temperatures. A small concrete deck adjacent to the pools makes getting in and out easier. The pools are big enough for three or four people, and are about 3 feet deep. The water temperature varies depending upon the time of year, but aver-

Alkali Hot Springs

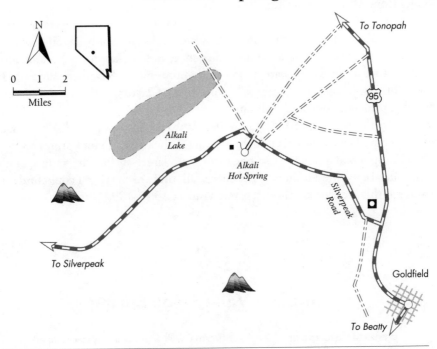

ages about 108 degrees F. in one, and 100 degrees F. in the other. The water is a little murky, but still makes a pleasant bath. The road passing by the springs is lightly traveled, but the pools are only a short distance from it, within sight. Use appropriate decorum. Alkali can be a popular place with locals on weekend nights, although there generally won't be anyone around on weekdays.

The Guisti Resort: Like so many other hot springs described in this book, Alkali was also a hot springs resort. Originally the hot springs consisted of only a few seeps, with little surface manifestation. In 1900, however, the Combination Mines Company drilled a substantial hole into the side of the hill to draw out more of the water. The water was concentrated in a channel and piped all the way to Goldfield, to be utilized in the company's mill. During Goldfield's heyday in the early 1900s, the springs were developed into a thriving resort. The spa contained a large swimming pool (which lies in ruins today), a large bathhouse, and several outbuildings. The spa was mostly patronized by folks from Goldfield, although travelers from other areas were known to visit. If you look closely you can see many hints of this long-since deserted resort.

Other hot springs in the area: The nearby town of Silverpeak, about 18 miles from Alkali Hot Spring, contains one small hot spring on the north side of town, immediately off Nevada Highway 265. The hot springs were reportedly used for the town's water supply. The Waterworks Hot Spring (as Silverpeak's springs were once known) are quite radioactive, and perhaps for this reason are not a source of the town's water today. The community of Silverpeak supports a large lithium mine in adjacent Clayton Valley. Clayton Valley is one of the world's principal sources of lithium.

On the east side of Clayton Valley, between Silverpeak and Alkali, hot springs have been reported at different times. Labeled Pearl Hot Springs on the USGS topographic map, these hot springs are largely below the surface, and have surface manifestation only during certain times of the year. I could find no water at this location on three separate visits in 1991, 1993, and 1996.

38

Fish Lake Valley Hot Spring

General description: A large geothermal well, from which water is piped into a large concrete pool, overflowing into several warm ponds in an isolated portion of central Nevada. Owned by Esmerelda County, these hot springs have been improved over the years but have also seen substantially increased use and, with it, damage.

Location: Central Nevada, about 70 miles southwest of Tonopah.

Primitive/developed: Primitive by location only. The hot water has been piped into a fancy, brand-new pool.

Best time of year: Fall or spring. Summer can be hot, and the road can be wet during winter.

Restrictions: Please help keep this place from being bulldozed by removing trash and refraining from vandalism.

Access: Most sturdy passenger cars can make the trip. Four-wheel drive may be required in wet periods, and the road can become completely washed out in flash floods.

Water temperature: About 105 degrees F. in the tub, overflowing into several lukewarm ponds.

Nearby attractions: The ghost towns of Candelaria and Basalt.

Services: None; the nearest gasoline, food, and lodging can be found in Tonopah, 70 miles away. You can also drive to Bishop, California, about 80 miles west on U.S. Highway 6.

Camping: Undeveloped camping is permitted at the hot spring. Keep in mind that there is no water or toilets here, however, and you may be sharing the area with others.

Map: USGS Davis Mountain, NV quadrangle (7.5 minute scale).

Finding the spring: From Tonopah, travel west on U.S. Highway 6 for 41 miles to Coaldale Junction. Stay on US 6 (left) and continue another 6 miles to Nevada Highway 773 where you turn left (south). Drive south on NV 773 for 9 miles, connecting with Nevada Highway 264. Go about 5.7 miles south from the intersection of NV 773 and NV 264, and turn left onto a graded dirt road (immediately before a small house). Drive on this graded road for about 5.8 miles, then bear left at a Y in the road. Drive another 1.2 miles to the spring.

The hot spring: Discovered in 1970 by an oil-exploration well, the hot water at Fish Lake Valley has been an excellent place to bathe ever since. The large-volume hot water well is piped into a large concrete pool complete with wooden benches and a large concrete patio. The pool is about 7 feet by 2 feet and about 3 feet deep. The water overflows into two warm ponds, which now contain goldfish, and the pool's water is clean and very appealing. The spring has been improved over the years by the county, with fences, barbecue pits, and trash cans all put up in the last few years.

Fish Lake Valley Hot Spring.

Fish Lake Valley Hot Spring

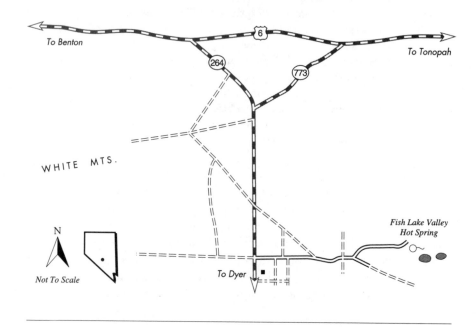

A few years ago the well was not widely known, and due to its rather isolated location made for a pleasant, private desert hot spring experience. The increase in use of the spring has brought the usual ramifications—trash, vandalism, alcohol abuse, and other assorted problems. Several signs remind visitors that if these types of problems do not cease, the spring will be closed (and probably bulldozed). Generally, however, this is still a pleasant place to visit, and is certainly a great place for a hot bath.

There are other hot wells reported in the Fish Lake Valley, although none of these have any bathing opportunities at present. The area does seem to have substantial geothermal potential, although most of it is below the surface.

SOUTHERN NEVADA

Dominated by Las Vegas in the south, southern Nevada possesses some of the most beautiful and desolate country in the state. Although the military owns and operates a large portion of the region, there is ample space to explore. As with other portions of Nevada, much of the land is owned by the Bureau of Land Management. There are few towns once you get away from Las Vegas, so plan ahead if you plan on venturing out. Also be aware that this part of the state can be significantly hotter than the other regions discussed so far. You may want to avoid this area during the heat of summer.

Many springs in this region are a short trip from Las Vegas and are worth visiting if you're staying in the big city. Four of the hot springs profiled in this section are within Lake Mead National Recreation Area, and tend to see more visitors than others described in the book. To reach the three hot springs downriver from Hoover Dam, we recommend taking a boat trip. Although you can hike to two of the springs, one of the hikes is difficult and the other is even worse. If you rent a boat at Willow Beach, you can reach the springs relatively easily by water.

DEATH VALLEY REGION

A few hours from Las Vegas, the Death Valley area is bordered on the west by Death Valley National Park, and on the east by Nellis Air Force Base. The region is bisected by U.S. Highway 95, connecting it to Tonopah to the north and Las Vegas to the south. The mostly dry Amargosa River runs from mountains within Nellis A.F.B., through Beatty, and eventually into Death Valley itself at Badwater, the lowest spot in the United States at 282 feet below sea level. Several ghost towns dot the area, including Rhyolite, Bullfrog, and Amargosa. A few hot springs in California can be reached from this region, although distances in this area are far and towns are few. The semi-resort town of Tecopa is about 80 miles southeast. The hot springs in Saline Valley can be reached via a long drive on paved highway plus a longer drive on dirt roads. Dirty Socks Hot Spring is farther west beyond the turnoff for Saline Valley on California Highway 190, about 105 miles from Beatty.

39

Bailey's Hot Springs

General description: A rustic hot spring resort with three separate gravel-bottom pools outside a small town.

Location: Southwestern Nevada, immediately north of the town of Beatty, about 115 miles northwest of Las Vegas.

Primitive/developed: Developed, but not fancy.

Best time of year: Fall, winter, or spring. Summer is hot, and bathing in even an indoor hot spring may not be appealing

Restrictions: This is a private resort, so tubs must be rented to use.

Access: The resort is immediately off the highway, so any car can make the trip.

Water temperature: Varies from 100 to 108 degrees F. depending upon the pool chosen.

Nearby attractions: The ghost towns of Rhyolite and Bullfrog.

Services: There are no services at the resort, but basic services can be found 5 miles away in Beatty.

Bailey's Hot Springs

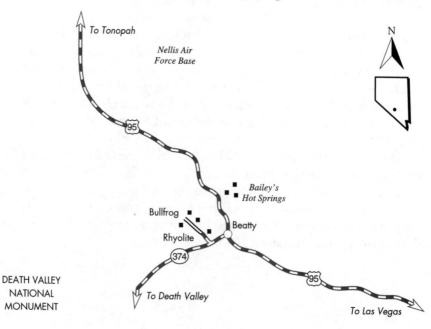

To Tonopah

Nellis Air
Force Base

N

95

Bailey's
Hot Springs

Bullfrog

Beatty

Rhyolite

374

DEATH VALLEY
NATIONAL
MONUMENT

To Death Valley

95

To Las Vegas

Camping: Spaces can be rented for tents or RV camping. Pool use is free to those camping at the resort.

Map: Nevada State Highway map.

Finding the spring: From Las Vegas travel north on U.S. Highway 95 for 115 miles to the town of Beatty. Continue north out of town about 5 miles to the resort on the right side of the highway. From Tonopah, travel south on US 95 for 87 miles to the resort on the left side of the highway. From Death Valley National Park, drive east on California Highway 190, which becomes Nevada Highway 374, to the town of Beatty. Turn left on US 95 and go 5 miles to the resort.

The hot springs: This simple, unadorned hot spring facility is supplied by several natural hot springs, each with substantial flow and temperature. The hot spring water is diverted into three pools at Bailey's, each covered and private. The water is piped into each room where it is kept clean by sufficient flow. The pools are all large, with sandy bottoms. Pool use is free to fee campers and open to the public for a small fee ($3 in 1995).

The towns of Rhyolite and Bullfrog are immediately west of Beatty off NV 374. Follow signs from town, taking a dirt road about 3 miles from the highway.

LOWER COLORADO RIVER

The narrow Black Canyon below the mighty Hoover Dam is home to three delightful hot springs. All the springs are excellent for bathing, and all can be reached relatively easily by boat. Although two of the springs are located in Nevada and the third is in Arizona, they are all in the same vicinity. Since these springs are within the Lake Mead National Recreation Area, stop in at one of the ranger stations for further information, including up-to-date weather information, access issues, and regulations. The most convenient station to visit is the Alan Bible Visitor Center, (702) 293-8906, at the intersection of U.S. Highway 93 and Nevada Highway 147 outside Boulder City. The visitor center is open daily from 8:30 a.m. to 4:30 p.m., but closed on Thanksgiving, Christmas, and New Year's Day. From the hot springs in the Lower Colorado River, an easy trip can be made to Rogers Warm Spring, on the west shore of Lake Mead.

Traveling in this region requires extra care and preparation. Thunderstorms can be particularly sudden and dangerous. Flash floods can strike with little warning. Be sure to check local weather forecasts and stay in town when storms threaten. Bring plenty of water, and do not take "shortcuts" on any of the hikes described. Always register at the visitor center, and never hike alone.

40

Gold Strike Hot Spring

(Also see map on page 117.)

General description: A picturesque hot spring in a fabulous narrow valley near the Colorado River. The spring can only be reached by a technically difficult hike, or by boat.

Location: Southern Nevada, about 7 miles southeast of Boulder City.

Primitive/developed: Primitive.

Best time of year: Fall, winter, or spring. Summer is too hot.

Restrictions: Check in at the Alan Bible Visitor Center and obtain information on trail condition, flash floods, and inclement weather.

Access: Getting to Gold Strike Hot Spring requires a 2-mile hike (one-way), which involves some boulder climbing. The trailhead can be reached by any vehicle. If you arrive by boat, you'll have to hike about 100 yards.

Water temperature: 110 degrees F. at source, varying in pools. The largest pool is about 100 degrees F.

Gold Strike Hot Spring

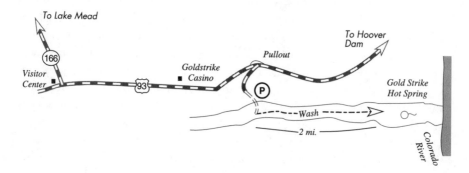

Gold Strike Hot Spring Canyon.

Nearby attractions: Hoover (Boulder) Dam, Lake Mead.

Services: None; the nearest gasoline, food, and lodging can be found in Boulder City, 7 miles away.

Camping: Camping is permitted in the canyon, but because the spring cannot be reached by car, all equipment must be packed in. Do not camp in the canyon if rain is approaching, since flash floods here can be deadly. Check in with the visitor center for latest camping information and requirements.

Map: USGS Boulder City, NV quadrangle (1:100,000 scale).

Finding the spring: From Boulder City, follow U.S. Highway 93 for about 3 miles to the Alan Bible Visitor Center at the intersection with Nevada Highway 166. Stop in here and check with the rangers regarding latest access information, and pick up a map. Continue on US 93 for 1.2 miles past the Gold Strike Inn and Casino to a paved turnoff on the right. This paved road is rather steep. If you don't think your vehicle can take it, park on the other side of the highway. About 30 feet down this paved road is the trailhead for the spring. The trail is not well marked, but just follow the wash downstream. The total hike is about 2 miles (one-way).

By boat, travel up the Colorado River (north) from Willow Beach toward Hoover Dam until you reach mile marker 62. Keep an eye out for a pit toilet on the left, which marks the entrance to the canyon with the hot spring. You will also be able to see a warning cable across the river from the mouth of the canyon.

The hot spring: Once you hike the 2 miles downcanyon you will begin to see water. The last half of the hike is the most difficult, requiring some boulder scrambling, with substantial dropoffs. You will eventually come to the hot spring sources. Continue down the canyon until you find a large pool that is ideal for bathing. There are also small waterfalls of hot water in this area, and several other smaller pools. If you wish, you can hike down to the river. Be careful, though, since there are many difficult parts to this trek, with steep dropoffs and rough terrain.

41

Boy Scout Hot Spring

General description: A spectacular hot spring in a narrow canyon, accessible only by boat. A short hike is required from the beach at the mouth of the canyon.

Location: Southern Nevada, on the Colorado River, about 10 miles from Willow Beach.

Primitive/developed: Primitive.

Best time of year: Year-round, though summers can be hot.

Restrictions: None.

Access: By boat only.

Water temperature: Varies by pool. Most are about 105 degrees F.

Nearby attractions: Boulder Dam, Lake Mead.

Services: None; the nearest gasoline, food, and lodging can be found in Boulder City, 20 miles away. Willow Beach has boat ramps, a store, and gasoline.

Camping: You can camp at the mouth of the canyon, but there is limited space. The river level also fluctuates widely, depending upon water released from the dam. Keep this in mind when securing your watercraft. It pays to check in with the Bureau of Reclamation for more details.

Map: USGS Boulder City, NV quadrangle (1:100,000 scale).

Finding the spring: To reach Willow Beach, travel east on U.S. Highway 93 from Boulder City. After crossing Hoover Dam, go south about 13 miles to the access road to Willow Beach, on the right. It is a short drive to the beach and marina. From Willow Beach, travel upstream by boat for 9 miles or so. The canyon with Boy Scout Hot Spring is a little

Gold Strike Hot Spring, Boy Scout Hot Spring, Arizona Hot Spring

more than 0.5 mile past mile marker 61. The canyon is on the left, immediately before the river makes a bend to the right. After securing your watercraft (keeping in mind fluctuating water levels), hike up the canyon for a few hundred yards to the first spring.

The hot springs: Another narrow canyon spring, Boy Scout Hot Spring is an excellent destination when boating the Colorado River. The hot spring sees a high volume of visitation during the prime boating season (May to October). Warm water trickles all the way to the river, but you will have to do some hiking in the creekbed to reach the hot springs. As you move farther upstream, the flow increases, as does the temperature. There are several pools ideal for bathing here, along with waterfalls larger than those in the Gold Strike Hot Spring Canyon. The size of these pools can vary widely, depending upon recent weather activities. As with the other canyons, be aware of flash floods and stay out if rain threatens.

42

Arizona Hot Spring

General description: The third hot spring along the Lower Colorado River, Arizona Hot Spring includes a waterfall and an excellent pool for bathing. It can be reached by boat or a 3.3-mile hike.

Location: Southern Nevada, about 12 miles southeast of Boulder City.

Primitive/developed: Primitive.

Best time of year: Year-round by boat. Avoid hiking into the spring in summer, since daytime air temperatures can exceed 110 degrees F.

Restrictions: None.

Access: Getting to this spring requires a boat ride and a small hike, or a 3.3-mile hike from the highway.

Water temperature: 110 degrees F. at source, decreasing as it flows downcanyon. At the waterfall the temperature is about 95 degrees F.

Nearby attractions: Hoover Dam, Lake Mead.

Services: None; the nearest gasoline, food, and lodging can be found in

Arizona Hot Spring

To Hoover Dam

8.4 Miles to Visitor Center

93

N

To Colorado River,
Arizona Hot Springs

White Rock
Canyon

Mile Marker 4.2
(4.2 Miles from Dam)

Sign

Parking
Area

To Kingman

Boulder City, 12 miles away. Willow Beach has boat ramps, a store, and gasoline.

Camping: There is plenty of open space at the mouth of the canyon where camping is permitted. There are no developed sites here, however, just lots of sand.

Map: USGS Boulder Dam, NV quadrangle (1:100,000 scale).

Finding the spring: From Boulder City, travel southeast on U.S. Highway 93 to Hoover Dam. Cross the dam and continue on US 93 to mile marker 4.2 and a National Park Service sign. Pull off the highway here, and park in the provided area. The hike begins here, at White Rock Canyon. Follow the main wash downstream for about 3 miles to the Colorado River. Once you reach the river, turn left (downstream) to the next canyon, less than 0.3 mile away. Hike the short distance up the canyon to the first pool.

If approaching by boat, travel upstream (north) from Willow Beach to mile marker 59. Go nearly another mile until you see warning buoys and a canyon on your right. There may also be a portable toilet at the mouth of the canyon. Secure your watercraft and hike the short distance to the spring.

The hot spring: Like other hot springs in this area, Arizona Hot Spring can be reached by boat, which means that, despite its relative isolation, it receives quite a few visitors. Because the hot spring water does not reach the Colorado River on the surface, the first pool you reach is one of the better soaking pools. As you follow the water up canyon you will reach other soaking pools, and eventually a large ladder that takes you up to other pools and waterfalls.

Hoover Dam: Built in 1935, Hoover Dam (originally called Boulder Dam) is one of the engineering marvels of the world. The reason for the dam's construction was threefold: to control the sometimes violent and unpredictable waters of the Colorado River; to provide hydroelectric power to cities in the Southwest; and to put thousands of unemployed Americans to work in the middle of the Great Depression. The construction successfully completed all of these goals.

Prior to the placement of the dam, steamboats actually navigated the waters of the Colorado River from its mouth in the Gulf of California. The large boats steamed upriver as far as Calville, a tiny hamlet of Mormon settlers. (The creation of the reservoir submerged the remains of the town.) To get that far, however, the steamboats utilized cable and pulley systems to drag themselves through oftentimes treacherous Black Canyon, where the hot springs listed above are located.

Dam construction took more than five years, requiring the labor of more than five thousand men and the capital of several large corporations. The growth of Las Vegas was aided in large part by the dam and its hydroelectric power; the infusion of money into the area; and the relative ease with which water could be drawn from the reservoir to support the city. Boulder City grew up as a supply center for the massive project, and remains a tourist supply center today.

Tours within the dam itself are conducted every day from 8 a.m. to 4:15 p.m., Memorial Day to Labor Day, and 9 a.m. to 4:15 p.m. the rest of the year. Admission is $3 for adults, $1.50 for seniors, and children are free.

LAKE MEAD REGION

Massive Lake Mead is a boaters' and anglers' paradise. The lake is more than 110 miles long, with a shoreline that curves for five times that distance. Although Nevada Highway 147 extends along the entire north shore of the lake, most of the rugged shoreline is accessible only by boat. The surrounding countryside is a rugged, dry landscape, offering panoramic vistas at every turn. Geologic formations add brilliant colors to the mountainsides.

Several recreation areas on the shoreline offer boat ramps, boat rentals, campgrounds, stores, and restaurants. Boat cruises can also be booked on the *Desert Princess*, a sternwheeler, by contacting Lake Mead Cruises at (702) 293-6180. For truly spectacular geologic formations and vistas, travel to the Valley of Fire State Park on Nevada Highway 169, east of Interstate 15. The park offers several points of interest and hiking trails. In addition, prehistoric rock art can be found in several park locations, including Atlatl Rock and Mouse's Tank. Because of its unusual rock formations and rare beauty, the Valley of Fire has been the scene of several movies and television commercials and shows. The park visitor center off NV 169 can be reached at (702) 397-2088. The center is open daily from 8:30 a.m. to 4:30 p.m., closed Christmas and New Year's Day.

43

Rogers Warm Spring

General description: A large and picturesque pond and small creek adjacent to Lake Mead within the Lake Mead National Recreation Area. This is a popular picnicking spot, not the best place for a private hot spring soak.

Location: Southern Nevada, about 50 miles northeast of Las Vegas.

Primitive/developed: There are picnic grounds, a parking lot, and restrooms. The pond itself is natural, although a small concrete dam has been built on one side.

Best time of year: Fall or spring. Summer is too hot, and winters can be too cold.

Restrictions: Rogers Warm Spring is within Lake Mead National Recreation Area, and is operated by the National Park Service. You must obey all park rules.

Access: Any car can make the trip, since the pond is just off a paved road.

Water temperature: 100 degrees F. at source, varying throughout the

Rogers Warm Spring

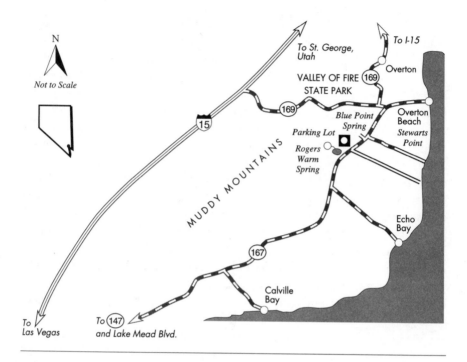

pond, which averages 90 degrees F. The water cools quickly as it flows out of the pond into the small creek.

Nearby attractions: Lake Mead, Valley of Fire State Park.

Services: None; the nearest gasoline, food, and lodging can be found in Las Vegas or Henderson, both 50 miles away. Some services can be found in Overton and Logandale, although these are small farming communities.

Camping: Camping is not permitted at Warm Spring. There are several developed and primitive campgrounds within Lake Mead National Recreation Area.

Map: USGS Lake Mead, NV quadrangle (1:100,000 scale).

Finding the spring: From Las Vegas, travel east on Lake Mead Boulevard. This road becomes Nevada Highway 147. Continue on NV 147 to Nevada Highway 167 (North Shore Drive). Turn left (east) here. Continue on NV 167 for about 27 miles to Rogers Warm Spring on your left. There will be a National Park Service sign for the picnic area and warm spring.

Rogers Warm Spring.

The hot spring: A natural hot spring forms this large pond in the middle of the desert, a few miles from Lake Mead. The water in the pond is pleasantly warm for bathing, although it has a murky and unappealing appearance. The water flows over a small concrete dam and forms a small creek. The small waterfall produced by this flow can be a nice spot for a bath if the weather is nice. Keep in mind that the water is not hot in the pond and rather lukewarm by the time it flows into the creek. Keep in mind also that this is a public picnic spot that receives many visitors. This is not a secluded spring. The National Park Service warns that bathers should not allow water into their noses, mouths, or ears, since a kind of amoeba that can be extremely dangerous has been found in the water. Follow this advice and do not put your head under water here.

44

Moapa Hot Springs

General description: A once-active but now defunct hot spring resort adjacent to the Moapa Indian Reservation near Las Vegas and Lake Mead. The springs were long used for bathing and irrigation, although there are currently no bathing opportunities.

Location: Southern Nevada, about 58 miles northeast of Las Vegas at the head of the Muddy River, 6 miles from Moapa.

Primitive/developed: Developed, but now defunct.

Best time of year: Fall, winter, or spring. Summer can be too hot.

Restrictions: This resort is private property and is closed at the time of publication. Do not trespass.

Access: Immediately off a paved road, any car can make the trip.

Water temperature: 90 degrees F.

Nearby attractions: Lake Mead, Valley of Fire State Park.

Services: None; the nearest gasoline, food, and lodging can be found in

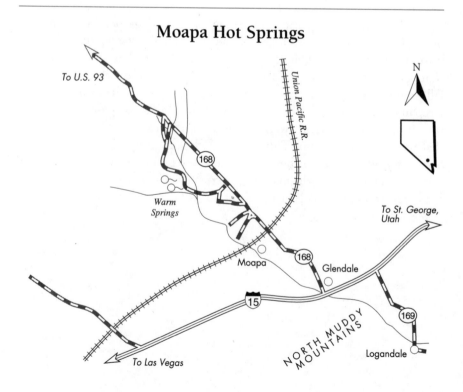

Moapa Hot Springs

Moapa Hot Spring.

Las Vegas, 58 miles away. A gas station, store, and restaurant can be found at the exit for Nevada Highway 168 off Interstate 15, 8.5 miles away.

Camping: Camping is not permitted at or near the resort, since most of the land in the immediate vicinity is privately owned. There are many developed and primitive campgrounds at Lake Mead National Recreation Area, 23 miles away.

Map: USGS Overton, AZ/NV quadrangle (1:100,000 scale).

Finding the spring: From Las Vegas travel east on Interstate 15 for 49 miles to Nevada Highway 168. Exit and travel north on NV 168 for 7.1 miles to a sign for "Warm Springs." Turn left here and follow this paved road 1.6 miles to the hot spring resort on your left.

The hot spring: Also known as Iverson's Warm Spring, this one-time lush resort is currently closed. A substantial warm spring exists within the property, producing substantial foliage on the grounds. The resort contains several buildings that are currently unused, and several large palm trees mark the property. Hopefully this resort in its scenic location will be reopened to the public in the near future. In contrast to the surrounding desert this resort is a lush oasis. Please respect the fence and do not trespass.

NORTHERN CALIFORNIA

Extending from Surprise Valley along the Nevada border in the east to the redwood country along U.S. Highway 101 in the west, northern California is a region of beauty and contrasts. Numerous mountain ranges cover the region, lifting most of the country to high elevation. In the north, the Cascades cover most of the eastern part of the state, with an abundance of volcanic activity. The Cascades are met at Lassen Volcanic National Park by the Sierra Nevada, which covers the southern two-thirds of the region. In the west Northern California is dominated by the Trinity and Siskiyou mountains, providing rugged backcountry largely controlled by the Forest Service.

Many people forget that much of California is only lightly populated and offers outdoor recreation aplenty. Although the Surprise Valley region is relatively dry, the rest of Northern California is much wetter than Nevada. Most of the springs described in this section are located in the high country and therefore are better visited during drier times of the year.

SURPRISE VALLEY REGION

The Surprise Valley is topographically similar to regions lying to its east, within the state of Nevada. Bounded on the west by the Warner Mountains, the valley lies within a rain shadow, and therefore is rather dry. The largest town, Cedarville, offers only basic services (gas, food). For more complete services, you must drive over the mountains into Alturas, 23 miles away.

The Surprise Valley is largely farming and cattle-raising country. The three lakebeds within the valley are generally dry, although in wetter years they will have a few feet of water in them. Numerous lakes and rivers abound in the surrounding mountains, offering fishing, hiking, and camping opportunities. Because of its relative lack of population and out-of-the-way location, Surprise Valley sees few visitors. The county road through the valley is not a major thoroughfare, and aside from California Highway 299 to Alturas, the few roads in the area are largely unimproved. For these reasons, you should find ample seclusion in this region.

45

Leonard's Hot Spring

General description: A series of ponds created by the damming of a creek of hot spring water in an isolated area. The remains of a hot springs resort, complete with empty swimming pool and collapsed buildings, can be seen adjacent to some of the ponds.

Location: Northeastern California, about 11 miles east of Cedarville.

Primitive/developed: Primitive, except for the damming of the creek and the remains of the resort.

Best time of year: Year-round. Roads may be muddy and slippery in wet weather.

Restrictions: None.

Access: Most passenger cars can make the trip.

Water temperature: 130 degrees F. at source, decreasing as it flows down the small creek. The most bathable pond is about 110 degrees F.

Nearby attractions: Eagleville Hot Spring, Surprise Valley Hot Springs.

Services: None; the nearest gasoline, food, and supplies can be found in Cedarville, 11 miles away. Cedarville is a small town, however, so do not

Leonard's Hot Spring.

Leonard's Hot Spring, Surprise Valley Hot Springs

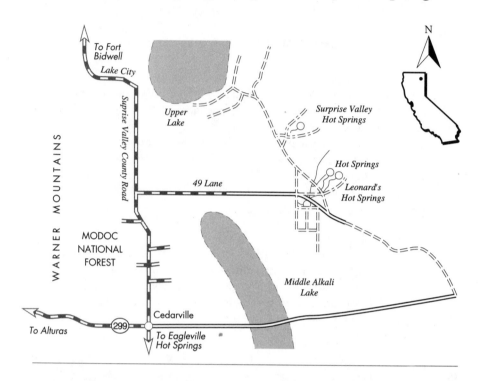

count on lodging there. Alturas, a slightly larger town, is 23 miles west on California Highway 299.

Camping: There do not appear to be any restrictions against camping at this spot. Please respect the privacy of others, pack out all trash, and keep in mind the several houses and ranches in the nearby valley.

Map: USGS Cedarville, CA quadrangle (1:100,000 scale).

Finding the spring: From Cedarville, travel north on Surprise Valley County Road (Nevada Highway 447 in Nevada) for about 5 miles to 49 Lane. Turn right (east) on this paved road and continue for about 6 miles; the road turns into a graded dirt road, but is well maintained. After about 6 miles, the road makes a major bend to the right. The springs are off to your left, along a small secondary dirt road.

The hot springs: Once you get to the secondary dirt road off of 49 Lane, drive less than 0.5 mile to the largest bathable pond. Follow the creek that is created by the hot spring water to find other ponds that have been constructed. Most of these are either too muddy or unappealing. If you follow the creek across the graded dirt road you will see the remains of the old hot springs resort.

There are some other, smaller ponds in which you can bathe on this side of the road. Most of these other ponds are rather shallow, however, and have silted up. The largest pond near the hot spring source is your best bet for a bath, at about 110 degrees F. The pond is about 3 by 5 feet, and 3 feet deep. Be careful before getting in, since the water temperature has a tendency to change.

This is a nice spot in a scenic valley in an underpopulated portion of northern California. On a weekday you can generally expect to have this spot to yourself. It gets a few visitors on weekends, however. Do keep in mind that you are not totally out in the middle of nowhere, and only a few miles from a town. Surprise Valley Hot Springs and Eagleville Hot Spring are relatively close by, and can be visited in the same day.

46

Surprise Valley Hot Springs

(See map on page 128.)

General description: Another series of ponds created by the damming of a creek of hot spring water near Leonard's Hot Spring.
Location: Northeastern California, about 11 miles from Cedarville.
Primitive/developed: Primitive, except for the damming of the creek.
Best time of year: Year-round. Roads may be muddy and slippery in wet weather.
Restrictions: None.
Access: Most passenger cars can make the trip. The secondary dirt road from 49 Lane to the springs is a little rough, and some low-clearance passenger cars may have problems.
Water temperature: 130 degrees F. at source, decreasing as it flows down the small creek. Average pond temperature is 110 to 115 degrees F.
Nearby attractions: Eagleville Hot Spring, Leonard's Hot Spring.
Services: None; the nearest gasoline, food, and supplies can be found in Cedarville, 11 miles away. Cedarville is a small town, however, so do not count on lodging there. Alturas, a slightly larger town, is 23 miles west on California Highway 299.
Camping: There do not appear to be any restrictions against camping at this spot. Please respect the privacy of others, pack out all trash, and keep in mind the several houses and ranches in the nearby valley.
Map: USGS Cedarville, CA quadrangle (1:100,000 scale).
Finding the springs: Follow 49 Lane as described for Leonard's Hot Spring (Spring 45). At the bend in the road, turn left (north). Follow this

Surprise Valley Hot Springs.

secondary dirt road for 0.75 mile until you see a small creek flowing under the road. Take the smaller dirt road on your right here, uphill. Follow this road for less than 100 yards to the various sources of hot spring water.

The hot springs: Similar to Leonard's Hot Spring (Spring 45), these springs are also rather primitive, and many are unappealing for soaking. Many of the springs are also much hotter than those at Leonard's, so you should be careful before entering any of them. There are several ponds in the creek that parallels the dirt road leading to the source. By the time the water crosses under the main road, however, it is a small trickle and there are no more bathing opportunities. As with Leonard's Hot Spring, many of these springs are unappealing due to silting, but with some selecting and perhaps some digging, you may find a good bathing spot.

47

Eagleville Hot Spring

General description: A fantastic hot spring in a scenic valley immediately off a seldom-used highway. Hot water emerging from the side of the hill is channeled into a small pond and large redwood hot tub.

Location: Northeastern California, about 22 miles from Cedarville.

Primitive/developed: Primitive, except for the piping of water into the pond and hot tub.

Best time of year: Year-round.

Restrictions: None.

Access: Any vehicle can get there, since the spring is immediately off a paved highway.

Water temperature: 130 degrees F. at source, about 110 degrees F. in the pond, and 105 degrees F. in the hot tub.

Nearby attractions: Leonard's Hot Spring, Surprise Valley Hot Springs.

Eagleville Hot Spring

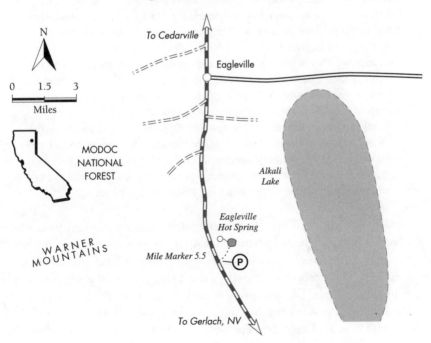

Eagleville Hot Spring.

Services: None; the nearest gasoline, food, and supplies can be found in Cedarville, 22 miles away, but do not count on lodging there. Eagleville has few or no services. Alturas, a slightly larger town, is about 45 miles west on California Highway 299.

Camping: This is not a place to camp, since the only parking is on the highway itself. There is plenty of public land in the surrounding countryside for undeveloped camping, however. Just be sure not to trespass.

Map: USGS Cedarville, CA quadrangle (1:100,000 scale).

Finding the spring: From the town of Cedarville, travel south on the county highway (Nevada Highway 447 in Nevada) 15 miles to the town of Eagleville. From Eagleville go another 7.5 miles south to a large turnout on the left side of the road. This turnout is immediately south of mile marker 5.50. Park here and walk the short but steep trail to the spring.

The hot spring: One of the better soaking opportunities in the area, Eagleville Hot Spring is in a beautiful location. It's also easy to get to and has an ideal water temperature. You will see the spring once you get out of your car at the turnout. The steep, slippery path to the spring is only 50 yards long, but be careful as you climb. The hot spring water emerges from the hill and is deposited into a small pond via tubing. This pond is about 10 feet across and 2 feet deep, with crystal-clear water. The water is also transported into a large redwood tub with slightly cooler water temperature than the pond. The tub is small but deep, with enough room for two.

The view from Eagleville Hot Spring is beautiful and, like so many described in this book, looks out on a vast valley flanked by mountain ranges. You can usually expect to have this spring to yourself, although it does seem to be known by those few who drive the county highway. If there is someone at the spring, you usually won't have to wait long to get it to yourself. On weekend nights local partygoers may hang here until late.

SOUTHERN CASCADE MOUNTAINS

Immediately west of the Surprise Valley lie the Warner Mountains and other ranges composing the Cascade Mountains. Within these mountains lies some of the best backcountry in the state of California, and some of the best hot springs. The Cascades, which extend into Oregon and Washington, border the Sierra Nevada to the south roughly at Lassen Volcanic National Park. Because the Cascades are an active chain of volcanoes, there is an abundance of hot spring activity within and adjacent to them. It is believed that the Sierra Nevada actually extend below the Cascades (which are younger), emerging again in northwestern California in the Trinity and Siskiyou regions.

Large parts of the area are controlled by the Forest Service, and therefore are unpopulated. The region is interspersed with several national monuments and national parks, offering abundant sightseeing and recreation. Roads in the region are few, although most areas have good access. Because these mountains can be quite high (well over 8,000 feet in places), winter travel is not recommended. Many of the roads described are subject to closure due to snow accumulation. Hiking, hunting, fishing, camping, and sightseeing opportunities are plentiful.

Prior to making any trip to the region, obtain a map. USGS topographic maps are excellent places to start. If you are entering a national forest, get the Forest Service map too. Be sure to contact the government agency in charge of the backcountry in which you propose to travel.

48

Kelly Hot Spring

General description: A closed hot spring resort that could be a pleasant place to enjoy the countryside and hot water. In a beautiful setting off the highway, Kelly is worth a look if you are in the area.

Location: Northern California, about 17 miles west of Alturas.

Primitive/developed: Developed. Although the resort is now closed, it was once a rustic hot springs resort with tub and pool rentals.

Best time of year: Spring, summer, or fall. The area receives substantial snow in winter.

Restrictions: This is private property, currently closed to the public. Perhaps one day it will reopen.

Access: Any vehicle can make the trip. Travel in the area is not advised during winter when the roads can be icy, snow covered, or closed altogether.

Water temperature: Unknown.

Nearby attractions: Lava Beds National Monument, Lassen Volcanic National Park.

Services: None; the nearest gasoline, food, and supplies can be found in

Kelly Hot Spring.

Kelly Hot Spring

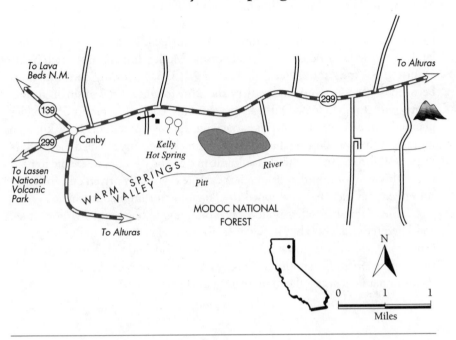

Alturas, 17 miles away. Some services can also be found in Canby, 2 miles west, although it is a much smaller town.

Camping: Camping is not permitted. There is a myriad of campgrounds in nearby Modoc National Forest, however. The closest campground is at Big Sage Reservoir, north of Alturas off Crowder Flat Road. Check with the Forest Service office in Alturas for further information.

Map: USGS Alturas, CA quadrangle (1:100,000 scale).

Finding the spring: From Alturas, travel west on California Highway 299 for 17 miles to a cluster of small buildings on your left. You will see an older building with a sign for Kelly Hot Spring.

The hot spring: Closed at the time of publication, this resort is in a beautiful location and has several hot springs on the premises. Perhaps the resort will reopen someday soon, or will be renovated by another owner. It has several manmade tubs into which the hot spring water has been diverted. Most of these tubs are in disrepair, but one can easily see the potential and appeal that this resort could have. Do not make a special trip to Kelly Hot Spring, but if you are in the area or traveling on California Highway 299, it is worth a stop to look at the old resort.

Lava Beds: About 50 miles northwast of Canby is Lava Beds National Monument. The monument is a huge lava field formed hundreds of years ago when nearby volcanoes spewed molten rock into the area. As the lava cooled, large caverns, deep chasms, and tunnels were formed. Because of this mazelike landscape, the Lava Beds were the site of the Modoc Indians' last-ditch battle against U.S. Army forces between 1872 and 1873. Following confrontations between the Modocs and local settlers, the army fought a series of small engagements with the Modocs. During a peace treaty council, a group of Modocs planned and carried out a surprise attack on the government officials, killing a number of them. Following the treacherous attack, the army pursued the Modocs in earnest, forcing them into this volcanic maze. The Modocs were able to hold out in this area for months, although they were eventually driven out, forced to surrender, and executed or shipped to Oklahoma for imprisonment.

The monument offers undeveloped camping, hiking trails, a visitor center, and interpretive displays but no services. To reach Lava Beds, travel north out of Canby on California Highway 139 to Toinessta Road, and follow the signs to the park, turning west. Go another 17 miles to the monument headquarters. For further information contact the monument staff at (916) 667-2282.

49

Healing Waters (Big Bend) Hot Springs Resort

General description: A series of hot springs on the banks of the Pit River, harnessed by a rustic resort. Several soaking opportunities range from concrete tubs to rock-lined pools in the river. The resort is under renovation, and the owners are building new tubs.

Location: Northern California, about 52 miles east of Redding.

Primitive/developed: Primitive, although some of the pools are manmade (concrete).

Best time of year: Year-round.

Restrictions: This is a private resort with pools open to guests only.

Access: Any vehicle can access the resort, which is located at the end of a paved road.

Water temperature: Ranging from 110 to 100 degrees F. depending on the tub chosen.

Nearby attractions: Lake Shasta, Lassen Volcanic National Park.

Services: The resort rents cabins. Gasoline, groceries, and food can be found in the town of Big Bend, 0.3 mile away.

Camping: There is camping at the resort, plus many campgrounds in nearby Trinity and Shasta national forests.

Map: California Highway Map.

Finding the springs: From the town of Redding, travel east on California Highway 299 for 35 miles to Big Bend Road, marked by signs for the town of Big Bend, where you turn left (north). Take this smaller paved road about 17 miles to Hot Springs Road, and turn left. Go to the end of this road (about 0.3 mile) to the hot springs resort. Hot Springs Road is the only left-hand turn in town.

The hot springs: Several hot springs in different locations feed this pleasant resort in a beautiful location. In the three manmade pools on the resort grounds the temperature is controlled by adding or subtracting river water. There are also several hot springs at the river's edge that have been channeled to form small pools. Here again river water can be added or subtracted to create the ideal temperature. Although this is not a secluded hot springs experience, you can generally have one of the pools to yourself and get some solitude. At about 2,000 feet elevation, the resort is low enough to avoid snow and is open year-round. Pools are open to guests at the cabins, and are generally open to day use for a fee.

Healing Waters Hot Springs Resort, Hunt Hot Springs

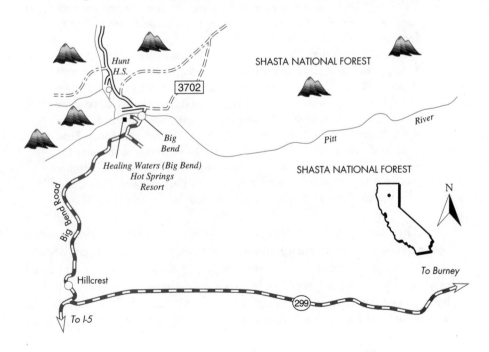

50

Hunt Hot Springs

General description: A series of small hot springs pools near Big Bend Hot Springs Resort. Adjacent to the Pit River, these pools are substantially less developed than those at Big Bend.

Location: Northern California, about 55 miles east of Redding.

Primitive/developed: Primitive, although some of the pools are manmade (concrete).

Best time of year: Year-round, but do not travel the rough dirt road to the spring when it is wet.

Restrictions: None.

Access: High-clearance vehicle required. You may need four-wheel drive when the road is wet.

Water temperature: Varies, depending upon the spring and pool chosen. Most pools average 105 degrees F.

Nearby attractions: Big Bend Hot Springs, Lake Shasta, Lassen Volcanic National Park.

Services: Cabins can be rented at the Big Bend Hot Springs, 2 miles away. Gasoline, groceries, and food can be found in the town of Big Bend, 1.8 miles away.

Camping: There do not appear to be any restrictions against undeveloped camping at this site. There are plenty of campsites in nearby Trinity and Lassen national forests.

Map: USGS McArthur, CA quadrangle (1:100,000 scale).

Finding the springs: From the town of Redding, travel east on California Highway 299 for 35 miles to Big Bend Road, marked by signs for the town of Big Bend, where you turn left (north). Take this smaller paved road for about 17 miles to the town of Big Bend. Continue on the same road through town, crossing the Pit River, for about 0.5 mile. You will pass Forest Road 3702 on the right. Continue straight for less than 0.25 mile to the next dirt road on the left. Take this road to a fork where you stay right. Go another mile to the road's end at the river. Do not try this road with a low-clearance vehicle. If the ground is wet, you will need four-wheel drive.

The hot springs: There are several choices at Hunt Hot Springs, from concrete pools on the riverbank to rock-lined pools in the river itself. Because these springs are located in a relatively underpopulated part of the state, and reached by a rough road, you should have a good chance at solitude. Your best bet is during the week. Nevertheless, the location is worth a visit. Although the water supplying the pools is hot, adding or subtracting creek water can regulate the temperature quite nicely. As always, be sure to pack out all trash and respect private property wherever you encounter it.

51

Terminal Geyser Hot Spring

General description: Two hot pools formed by a geyser in the high backcountry of northern California. A short hike is required to reach the hot springs.
Location: Northern California, about 20 miles north of Chester, surrounded by the Lassen Volcanic National Park.
Primitive/developed: Primitive, except for the creation of soaking pools.
Best time of year: Summer, early fall, or late spring. Snowfall makes the trail impassable.
Restrictions: None.

Terminal Geyser Hot Spring

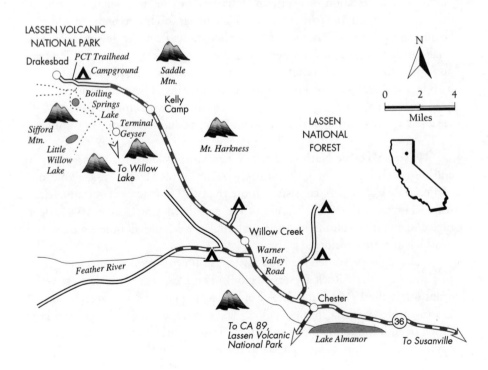

LASSEN VOLCANIC
NATIONAL PARK

Drakesbad   PCT Trailhead

Campground   Saddle
Mtn.

Boiling   Kelly
Springs   Camp
Lake
Terminal
Sifford   Geyser
Mtn.
Little   Mt. Harkness
Willow
Lake   To Willow
Lake

LASSEN
NATIONAL
FOREST

N

0   2   4

Miles

Willow Creek

Warner
Valley
Road

Feather River

Chester

To CA 89,   36
Lassen Volcanic
National Park   Lake Almanor   To Susanville

Access: Most passenger vehicles can reach the trailhead, unless the road is wet. You will have to hike 2.7 miles to get to the springs themselves.

Water temperature: Water cools from the geyser to 105 degrees F. and 100 degrees F. in the two pools.

Nearby attractions: Drakesbad Guest Ranch, Lassen Volcanic National Park.

Services: None; the nearest gasoline, food, and supplies can be found in Chester, 20 miles away. Drakesbad Guest Ranch, at the trailhead, rents rooms, but reservations must be made ahead of time. Call (916) 529-1512.

Camping: Check with Lassen Volcanic National Park for current camping rules and restrictions, since the springs are within the park boundaries. There are several campgrounds in the area.

Map: USGS Lake Almanor, CA quadrangle (1:100,000 scale).

Finding the spring: From Chester, travel northwest on Feather River Drive off California Highway 36. Take Feather River Dr. to Warner Valley Road and follow it for 17 miles to the Drakesbad Guest Ranch; the last few miles are dirt. At Drakesbad Ranch you will see the trailhead for the Pacific Crest Trail. Hike south on the trail, following signs to Great Boiling Lake and Terminal Geyser. It's about a 2.7-mile hike to the pools.

The hot spring: The two pools at Terminal Geyser are created from geyser runoff. The Lassen region is quite active volcanically, and Terminal Geyser is only one manifestation of geothermal activity in the area. There are several other hot springs in the park, most of which are far too hot to bathe in and can be quite hazardous. The hot spring water here flows from the geyser through a small gulch and into two different pools built for soaking purposes. The two pools are different temperatures, but both are pleasant. The pools are about 5 by 6 feet and 2 feet deep. The water is quite inviting. These are relatively isolated springs, so you will generally not have problems with crowds. But you will see a few visitors during peak hiking and backpacking season in late summer.

Lassen Volcanic National Park: When visiting Drakesbad Guest Ranch and Terminal Geyser Hot Spring you will be surrounded by the Lassen Volcanic National Park. The park consists of more than 100,000 acres of volcanic landscape. The most dominant feature of the park is Mount Lassen, 10,457 feet high and an active volcano itself. Several smaller volcanoes dot the region, most of which also are considered active.

The region is named for Peter Lassen, California pioneer, and rancher in this area (see Black Rock Desert Region). The Lassen area was last active in eruptions in the 1910s, but evidence of its sleeping power can be seen in countless fumaroles, boiling springs, boiling lakes, mudpots, hot springs, and lava flows. In addition to the many volcanic points of interest in the park, there are countless trails connecting travelers to backcountry lakes.

The park is open year-round, but because of high winter snowfall most roads are closed from late October to June. Winter activities (cross-country skiing, snowshoeing) can be enjoyed from Lassen Chalet, near the park's southern entrance on California Highway 89. Before venturing into the backcountry, contact park rangers for the latest information on wilderness permits, access, and other issues at (916) 595-4444.

NORTHERN SIERRA NEVADA

Geologically quite different than the Cascades to the north, the Sierra Nevada Range is similar in the fact that its peaks provide limitless high country recreation. The northern Sierras are also largely controlled by the Forest Service, limiting settlement in the region. Although the region is dotted with small towns and crisscrossed by paved and dirt roads, it is generally isolated, and visitors should take all precautions. High country travel is best done during spring, summer, and fall, since winter weather brings hazardous conditions. The only hot spring described for this region lies a relatively short distance from Reno, and can be an easy day trip from the little city.

52

Sierraville Hot Springs

General description: An unusual hot springs resort in a beautiful valley. The resort is a membership facility, but the tubs are generally open for lodge guests or day use. This is a clothing-optional facility.
Location: Northeastern California, 57 miles west of Reno.
Primitive/developed: Developed, while retaining a rustic feel.
Best time of year: Year-round.
Restrictions: This is a private, membership facility, but you can join on your first visit and rent tubs for day use.
Access: Any vehicle can make the short drive on the dirt road off the highway.
Water temperature: Varies, depending upon the tub chosen.
Nearby attractions: Plumas National Forest, the historic mining town of Downieville.
Services: Lodge rooms are available at Sierraville Hot Springs, along with a small restaurant. Gasoline and groceries can be found in Sierraville, a few miles away. Other accommodations can be found in Reno, 57 miles

away, or in Truckee, 25 miles away.

Camping: Campsites may be rented at Sierraville Hot Springs. There also are many developed and undeveloped Forest Service campgrounds in the area.

Map: California Highway Map.

Finding the springs: From Truckee, take California Highway 89 north for 25 miles to Sierraville. At the intersection of California Highways 89 and 49, take CA 49 to Lemon Canyon Road and turn right. Then turn right again on Campbell Hot Springs Road, adjacent to the airport. Follow this road to Sierraville Hot Springs.

The hot spring: Supplied by several natural hot springs, Sierraville Hot Springs Resort has harnessed them in unique ways. The resort has undergone several changes in the past few years, with many tubs recently renovated and improved. In a beautiful setting, almost all the tubs at the Sierraville resort offer a view of the surrounding valley. Guests can choose from several different tubs. There are several rooms with tubs inside that can be rented by the hour, offering a private soak, or redwood tubs on a wooden deck, large enough for six

Sierraville Hot Springs

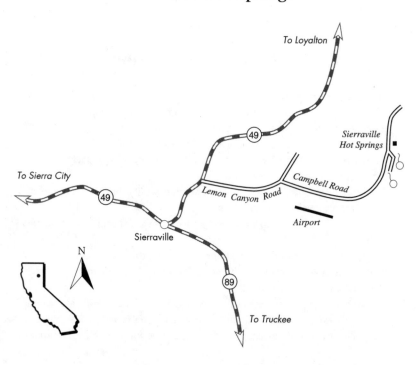

people. A communal area with a larger pool and several other tubs offers a choice for those who are less private. Keep in mind that this is a clothing-optional resort. If you are uncomfortable with public nudity, choose one of the private rooms.

MENDOCINO NATIONAL FOREST AND NORTHWESTERN CALIFORNIA

Mendocino National Forest lies within California's Coast Range, extending along the state's seacoast as far south as Ventura County. The Coast Range is made up of largely north-south trending mountains with rugged terrain. The range is significantly lower than either the Cascades or the Sierras, providing quite different flora and fauna. Dominated by scrub vegetation and occasional forests, the Coast Range is also quite drier than its larger neighbors. In places, however, the mountains are high enough to support forest biotas. Contact local land managing agencies before venturing out into Coast Range backcountry. The Mendocino National Forest office at Upper Lake can be contacted at (707) 275-2361.

53

Crabtree Hot Springs

General description: A group of natural hot springs dammed by volunteers into small, rock-lined soaking pools along a stream. As of this writing, the owners of Crabtree Hot Springs no longer allow public access to the hot springs. Do not trespass without the owners' specific permission.

Location: Northern California, near Clear Lake, about 20 miles north of Upper Lake.

Primitive/developed: Primitive, except for the damming of spring water into pools.

Best time of year: Spring, summer, and fall. Summer can be hot. During wet weather, roads may be impassable.

Restrictions: Public access to the hot springs, which are on private property, has recently been discontinued. Do not trespass without the owners' specific permission.

Access: The road into Crabtree Hot Springs is rough, and requires a high clearance vehicle and four-wheel drive, especially in wet weather. High water may make the road impassable.

Water temperature: 110 degrees F. at source, decreasing as the water flows into the pools. Average pool temperature is 100 degrees F.

Nearby attractions: Clear Lake.

Services: None; the nearest gasoline, food, and supplies can be found in Upper Lake, 20 miles away.

Camping: There do not appear to be any restrictions against camping in the vicinity of Crabtree Hot Springs. There are several Forest Service campgrounds in the area. Check with the Mendocino National Forest office in Upper Lake for more information. The springs themselves are on private property. Do not trespass without the owners' specific permission.

Map: USGS Lakeport, CA quadrangle (1:100,000 scale).

Finding the spring: Crabtree Hot Springs are reached from the town of Upper Lake. the springs are no longer accessible to the public.

Crabtree Hot Springs

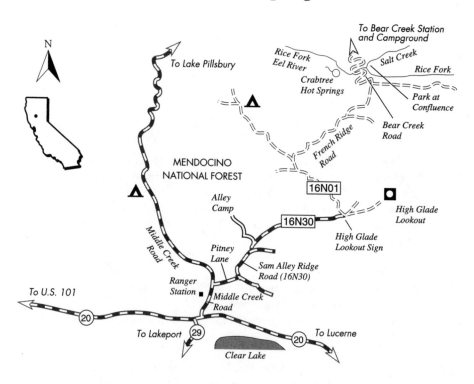

The hot spring: Crabtree is a great group of natural hot springs located on private property within Mendocino National Forest. The several hot springs here have been dammed into three soaking pools, one of them strengthened with concrete and rock. The springs are relatively close to each other along Bear Creek, which usually has water in it. The pools average about 100 degrees F., and are large enough to accommodate at least five people. There is a fairly large swimming hole in the adjacent creek.

Although difficult to get to over the rough and sometimes impassable French Ridge Road, Crabtree Hot Springs once saw a fairly large number of visitors. Weekdays in spring or fall were the best times to visit for those seeking solitude. The owners have recently discontinued public access, however. Please do not visit the hot springs without specific permission from the owners, and obey all "no trespassing" signs.

54

Vichy Springs Resort

General description: A peaceful, historically significant resort complete with a variety of warm pools, massage services, full breakfast, and acres of property to explore, including a creek and a waterfall.

Location: Northwestern California, immediately outside the town of Ukiah.

Primitive/developed: Developed, except for the waterfall and land surrounding the ranch.

Best time of year: Year-round.

Restrictions: This is a private resort, with pools open only to guests or day users who pay a small charge. Contact the resort ahead of time for reservations.

Access: Any vehicle.

Water temperature: 90 degrees F. at source; varying depending upon pool chosen. Water is heated to about 105 degrees F. in one pool.

Nearby attractions: Clear Lake, Pacific Coast, Sonoma, Napa wine country.

Services: The resort offers cottages and lodge rooms along with a full breakfast. All other services can be found in Ukiah, 3 miles away.

Camping: Camping is not permitted at the resort, but several locations can be found within a few hours' drive.

Map: California State Highway map.

Finding the spring: From U.S. Highway 101, exit onto Vichy Springs Road in the town of Ukiah. Travel east of town on Vichy Springs Rd. for slightly less than 3 miles, following National Historic Landmark signs pointing you to the resort.

The hot springs: The Vichy Springs Resort and Inn is a historic landmark set in the front of a sprawling, 700-acre ranch. The current owners of this beautiful property have expended a great deal of time and energy into renovating the resort, while maintaining its historic character. Almost all the buildings at Vichy are original, and all retain their historic integrity. Boasting the state's only naturally effervescent spring, Vichy feeds hot water from the spring into a series of small, bathtub-shaped pools for single or double use. The spring's source, the pride of the resort, produces about 100 gallons of water per minute. One of the most unusual aspects of the spring is the fact that it is naturally carbonated, the only one of its kind in the country. Bathtub pools can be enjoyed outside or within a small structure sheltering the tubs from the weather, two tubs to a

Vichy Springs Resort

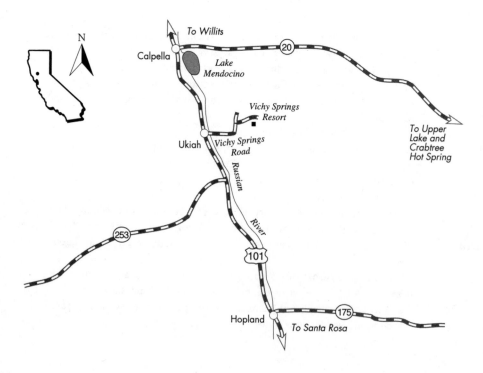

Chemisal Falls a half hour walk upstream on the Vichy Springs Ranch.

room. Vichy water is also fed into a large, warm swimming pool and a modern Jacuzzi-style tub where the temperature is raised to about 105 degrees F.

Many people swear by the curative benefits of the natural hot spring water here. The water is high in calcium carbonate and boron, so it tends to soften your skin considerably. Along with the various baths, massages can also be obtained. A waterfall is accessible via a short hike, open to all guests and day-users of the resort. Bathing in the waterfall is an equally invigorating experience on a warm day. Phone ahead for more information and reservations, (707) 462-9515.

A historic resort: Constructed originally in 1854, Vichy Springs is the oldest continuously operating mineral water resort in California. Named after natural mineral springs in France, whose chemistries are strikingly similar, the Vichy resort is a historical treasure. The first developer of the property was William Day, who built several cabins, a bathhouse, baths, and a dining room by 1861. In 1867 the resort passed into the hands of William Doolan, who operated it for the next thirty years, building the first large swimming pool on the property. During Doolan's ownership, the springs became a popular destination for the rich and famous. Such celebrities as Ulysses S. Grant, William Harrison, Mark Twain, Jack London, and Grace Hudson, among others, visited the springs.

Hot Pool with replica of Monet's Bridge crossing Vichy Creek.

Following another change of ownership, the resort was bought by A. F. Redemeyer in 1901. Redemeyer leased the operation of the resort to others, including Bob Jones in 1914. Jones remodeled portions of the resort and undertook additional construction measures, including an auto garage, a lounge, a lobby, and a double bowling alley (much of which still remains today). Following the Great Depression of the 1930s, the resort fell into disuse and decline until the current owners bought it in 1977. Gilbert and Marjorie Ashoff acquired the property to bottle the water, but soon got to work on remodeling the resort. Since the resort buildings and grounds were in disrepair, a great deal of effort was expended to update the buildings without removing their historic feel. Following a variety of bureaucratic roadblocks, lawsuits, and obstructions, the Ashoffs succeeded in renovating the resort. The baths and buildings awaiting you at Vichy are basically unchanged from the original resort of the 1860s. Vichy Hot Springs is definitely worth a visit.

CENTRAL CALIFORNIA

Central California as defined here is another area of contrasts. In the east, the region is dominated by the Sierra Nevada. The mountains slope gradually upward from the west to their peak elevations before dropping off rapidly to the east. U.S. Highway 395 serves as a lifeline to the eastern side of the mountains, providing access into the backcountry and connecting California with Nevada. As the mountains drop rapidly, the highway opens to spectacular scenery. The highest point in the state, Mount Whitney, at 14,494 feet, is a short distance away from the small town of Lone Pine, sitting on the Owens Valley floor.

Within the high Sierras attractions abound, the most popular being Yosemite National Park, accessed from the east on California Highway 120. Several other national and state parks and monuments exist in this portion of the Sierras. Since the year-round population of this region is light, there is outdoor recreation aplenty. During winter months, most roads leading into the mountains are closed due to snowfall. The best time to enjoy the Sierras is in summer, and portions of fall and spring.

West of the mountains is the Great or Central Valley, California's agricultural heartland. Beyond the Great Valley the elevation rises again in the Coast Range before meeting the Pacific Ocean. Much of the country within the Coast Range is rugged and unpopulated. Central California also contains some of the most inhospitable desert in the country. Death Valley National Monument, recently expanded to include portions of other ranges and valleys, is perhaps the best-known desert region of the state. The thousands of acres within this national monument are completely devoid of people and hardly see human visitation.

The main thoroughfares through central California are north-south trending, following the contours of the state. Interstate 5 connects California with Oregon and points north, and is the fastest way to traverse the state. U.S. Highway 101 lies to the west, connecting many of the larger towns and is a more scenic route.

CARSON RIVER AREA

Originating in the high Sierra Nevada, the Carson River extends into Nevada, eventually terminating in Lahontan Reservoir. The river was named for famed mountain man, explorer, and trailblazer Christopher "Kit" Carson, who first recognized it as a travel corridor through Nevada and entryway to the high country. The Carson River Route became one of the most popular paths into California for the emigrants of the 1840s, 1850s, and 1860s.

Today the area offers hunting, fishing, hiking, and camping among other outdoor activities, ranging from the high country around Grover Hot Springs to lower elevations near the Carson River Hot Springs and the state line. The two hot springs listed here for this region are quite different, one a collection of largely unaltered springs at the end of a difficult road on the East Carson River, the other harnessed for use in a campground swimming pool. Because of high elevations at Grover Hot Springs, winter driving is not advised, particularly during storms.

55

Carson River Hot Springs

General description: Two sets of natural hot springs on the East Carson River, far from civilization and requiring either a raft trip or a grueling drive.
Location: Eastern California, about 20 miles southwest of Gardnerville, Nevada.
Primitive/developed: Primitive.
Best time of year: Summer, spring, or fall. The road may be impassable during periods of snow and rain.
Restrictions: Although located on national forest land, the road to these springs passes through private property. Access is generally granted, however.
Access: You will need a high-clearance vehicle at the least, and four-wheel drive is highly recommended. Do not try this road with any vehicle in wet weather.
Water temperature: The water emerges from the source at about 105 degrees F., and cools depending upon the amount of river water admitted to the pools.
Nearby attractions: Carson River.
Services: None; the nearest food, gasoline, and lodging can be found in Gardnerville, 20 miles away.

Camping: Camping is permitted, although there are no developed sites. Contact Toiyabe National Forest for up-to-date rules and restrictions.
Map: Toiyabe National Forest, California.
Finding the spring: From Carson City, travel south on U.S. Highway 395 for 11 miles to Gardnerville. Continue south on US 395 for 12 miles to the Leviathan Mine Road on your right (west). Turn right here and go about 1.7 miles to Forest Road 189, where you should turn right. Take this increasingly smaller and less maintained road about 3.8 miles to a fork in the road. Continue straight ahead at this fork. Pass through a cattle gate (closing it behind you) and drive another 4 miles to the East Carson River. Park here, cross the river, and walk the last 50 yards to the springs on the other side. The second set of hot springs is about 0.5 mile upstream from the first set. Hike to this spring, since crossing the river can be difficult and the road gets worse on the other side. If you wish to arrive at these springs by raft instead of by car, contact one of the many river rafting guide companies operating in the area. Do not try the trip by yourself.

The hot springs: Both sets of hot springs are on the bank of the East Carson River, and each provides excellent bathing opportunities. Both pools

Carson River Hot Springs

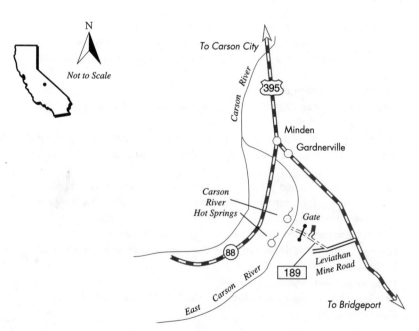

have been dug out of the soil by volunteers and are kept up by continuous digging and placement of rocks as they wash out. Although difficult to reach by car, the hot springs are relatively popular and well-known. During rafting season (May to August) most guided trips stop and visit the springs. The road you take to the springs passes through private property, but to date the landowner has allowed access. Be sure to respect posted signs.

Come prepared on this trip, since the road is quite difficult. Bring plenty of food and water, a spare tire with sufficient air in it, a car jack, and plenty of tools. Also, let someone know that you are going and when you expect to be back.

56

Grover Hot Springs

General description: A state-run hot springs park with a communal warm pool, adjacent to a campground in the high Sierra.

Location: Eastern California, outside the small town of Markleeville and about 38 miles southwest of Carson City.

Primitive/developed: Developed.

Best time of year: Year-round, except in heavy snowfall. The campground is closed from October to May.

Restrictions: This is a state park, so all rules and regulations must be obeyed. The pool is limited to fifty people at any given time. Park hours vary, depending upon the time of year. Phone ahead for rules and regulations, (916) 694-2248.

Access: Any vehicle can access the park, since it is on a paved highway. Roads may be closed during winter, particularly during storms.

Water temperature: About 148 degrees F at its source. The hot water is cooled to about 100 degrees F in the pool.

Nearby attractions: Hot Springs Trail, Burnside Lake.

Services: Some services can be found in nearby Markleeville. With complete services, Minden and Gardnerville are 20 miles away.

Camping: There is a campground at the park. Get reservations ahead of time since it fills up quickly. Reservations can be made through MISTIX at 1-800-444-PARK.

Map: California State Highway map.

Finding the springs: From the town of Gardnerville travel southwest on U.S. Highway 88 for about 15 miles to Woodfords and the California Highway 89 intersection. Turn left and go south, about 5 miles, to the town of

Markleeville and exit, right, on Hot Springs Rd. Follow Hot Springs Rd. about 3 miles to the Grover Hot Springs State Park entrance station.

The hot springs: The large, communal warm pool is quite pleasant despite the usual crowds. The occupancy limit of the pool is fifty people, so you may have to wait until someone else leaves before you can go in. The natural source of the pool is uphill a few yards. The water is treated, and flushed constantly, maintaining a constant temperature.

The park is open year-round offering vacationers access to a hot soak throughout the year. The park lies at 6,000 feet elevation, so summers are generally mild (in the 80s). Winters can be very cold, however, and the road occasionally will be closed due to snowstorms. The springs are especially enjoyable in winter, when steam wafting from the large pool creates a surrealistic look. The water also feels that much better when the air temperature is in the 40s and 50s.

The park offers campsites and several interesting hikes. A particularly enjoyable hike is the Hot Springs Creek Trail, leading you to a waterfall and, eventually, to Burnside Lake. Trail maps can be obtained at the park. For further information contact the park at (916) 694-2248.

Grover Hot Springs

Eastern Sierra—
The Hot Springs Jackpot!

Lying along the base of the Sierras, U.S. Highway 395 south of Carson City provides access to some of the best hot springs country in the nation. From north of Bridgeport to south of Lone Pine, hot springs of all types abound. Most of these springs are completely natural, with just enough alterations made to provide bathing opportunities. A few have been partially or totally harnessed. The springs described in this region are all excellent bathing springs, and you could spend weeks sampling them all.

Because US 395 sees a substantial amount of traffic, many of these springs are well known. Seclusion can be had, however, particularly off-season and during the week. On weekends and particularly holidays, the springs see heavy visitation. Several towns dot the landscape, providing ample services along the way.

US 395 allows easy access to a variety of attractions, from low deserts in the east to alpine mountains in the west. The numerous creeks and rivers draining the Sierras offer countless fishing opportunities. Mono Lake is a birders paradise. Cross-country and downhill skiers will love the Mammoth Lakes region. Camping and hiking can be enjoyed year-round. The region is also rich in history, and only a little extra time is needed to enjoy this aspect of the area.

57

Fales Hot Springs

General description: A closed resort with several unfinished pools and structures. Currently off-limits to bathing, it may someday reopen. A small natural pool downstream a few hundred yards has been accessible to the public in the past. Recently, "no trespassing" signs have blocked access to this pool also.
Location: Eastern California, immediately off U.S. Highway 395, about 13 miles north of Bridgeport.
Primitive/developed: Developed, although the resort is now closed and in disrepair.
Best time of year: Summer, spring, or fall. US 395 may be difficult or impassable during winter storms.
Restrictions: The resort itself is on public land, but several "no trespass-

Fales Hot Springs

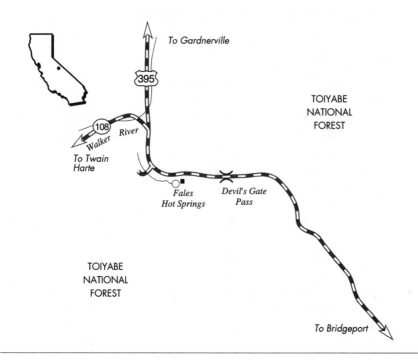

ing" signs have been posted. There is private property behind the resort, which should be respected.

Access: Any vehicle can get to Fales, immediately off US 395. The road can be treacherous during winter storms.

Water temperature: 150+ degrees F. at the source, cooling rapidly as it flows down the creek.

Nearby attractions: Mono Lake, Yosemite National Park.

Services: None, but services can be found in Bridgeport, 13 miles away.

Camping: No camping allowed. This is not a good place to camp anyway, since it is immediately off the highway. There are several Forest Service campgrounds in the vicinity, including two a few miles north on US 395.

Map: California State Highway map.

Finding the springs: From Bridgeport, travel north on U.S. Highway 395 for 13 miles to the ruins of the resort on your left. A pool in the small ditch could once be accessed a few hundred yards farther north along the highway from a second turnout in the road. The pool is a short distance downhill from the turnout.

The hot springs: Fales Hot Spring was at one time a substantial resort, as is apparent from the large pools, buildings, and individual rooms now in disuse. The water at the source is extremely hot! DO NOT GO NEAR THIS WATER—it could be fatal. Follow the hot spring water as it flows into a small stream near several individual rooms. These individual bathhouses were constructed with local stone and cement over the stream in which the hot water flows. Water could be diverted into the rooms, providing the best soaking opportunities, although the rooms are now dry.

The hot creek water forms a nice-sized pool for soaking a few hundred yards downstream. The temperature in this pool is about 95 degrees F., and was in the past accessible to the public. Several "no trespassing" signs have been posted recently, however, closing yet another spring to public use.

Fales history: The hot springs at Fales originally were used as a way station on a toll road in the 1870s. In 1878, the first direct route between San Francisco and Bodie was completed with the Sonora-Mono Wagon Road. The road was a passenger and freight route from the productive mines at Bodie to markets in San Francisco. It followed the Stanislaus River, then an old Indian trail over the pass to Leavitt Meadows, then to Fales and Bridgeport, and finally

Fales Hot Springs.

to Bodie. Some facilities were constructed at Fales during this time period, but the resort aspect of the spring was developed later. Several small bathhouses and a lodge were built. But this enterprise largely failed, and the resort fell into disuse.

Another more recent attempt was made to reopen the hot springs resort, but it never fully materialized. Foundations for a large swimming pool were laid out, and a few improvements were made to some of the buildings, none of which were ever finished. Time will tell what becomes of this fascinating historic location and its high-temperature hot springs.

58

Travertine Hot Springs

General description: A series of natural hot springs, bolstered to provide several bathing opportunities. Popular in the Eastern Sierras, Travertine Hot Springs are most notable because of the multicolored travertine formations associated with the pools.

Location: Eastern California, 2 miles south of Bridgeport.

Primitive/developed: Primitive, although several pools have been dug to provide better soaking opportunities, and one has been cemented in.

Best time of year: Year-round. The road to the springs may be impassable in wet weather.

Restrictions: None.

Access: Although a high-clearance vehicle is best, most standard vehicles can make the short drive to the springs. During wet weather you will need four-wheel drive.

Water temperature: Varies depending upon source. Most average 130 degrees F. Several pools range from 90 to 110 degrees F.

Nearby attractions: Twin Lakes, Bodie, Buckeye Hot Springs.

Services: None, but services can be found 2 miles away in Bridgeport.

Camping: Undeveloped camping is allowed at the springs. Since this is a popular spot, respect the privacy of others. Do not monopolize the springs by camping immediately next to any of the pools. There also are several Forest Service campgrounds in the area. Check at the local ranger station for details.

Map: USGS Bridgeport, CA quadrangle (1:100,000 scale).

Finding the springs: From Bridgeport, travel south on U.S. Highway 395 about 0.5 mile and turn left on Jack Sawyer Road, a few hundred yards before the ranger station. Drive on this paved road for 0.3 mile to where

Travertine Hot Springs

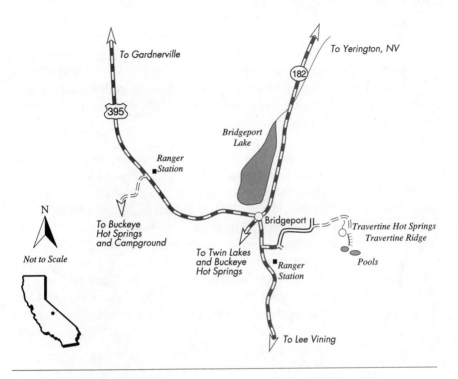

the road begins to bend to the right; turn left on a dirt road here. Follow this dirt road for about 1.2 miles, staying right at the first Y in the road. You will drive over some rough spots where the road has been washed out, but it's only a short segment. As you approach the top of the hill you will see the multicolored travertine of the hot springs. Drive until you reach the top cement pool. From here follow the ridge of travertine down to the other pools. Do not try to drive next to the lower pools, since the ground is very muddy in places.

The hot springs: Travertine Hot Springs offers several soaking opportunities and presents intriguing geology in a beautiful setting. The upper hot spring (the first you come to) has a small concrete pool built adjacent to it. This pool presents the best soaking opportunity, since it is about 105 degrees F. and shaped like a bathtub. It's also the most popular spring, however.

The lower pools are formed from water dripping off the ridge of travertine into small, crude pools constructed by hot springs users. There are several of these pools, ranging in temperature from 105 to 90 degrees F., and all are only a foot or two deep. The water is also a little murky here, but who cares? The view is fantastic.

As always, respect others' privacy and do not leave any trash behind. So far this spring has stayed free from trash and open. Let's keep it that way.

Nearby Twin Lakes offers lake and stream fishing, camping, and hiking. The resort provides a complete marina, boat rentals, general store, and RV park. On the road to Twin Lakes, Doc and Al's Resort provides cabins and camping, with excellent creek fishing. To reach Twin Lakes, travel west of Bridgeport on Twin Lakes Road for about 15 miles.

Bodie: Southeast of Bridgeport in the dry sage country lies the ghost town of Bodie. Run by the California State Parks Department and a cadre of dedicated volunteers, Bodie is maintained in a state of "arrested decay" to give visitors a glimpse of what the old town looked and felt like in the 1880s.

Gold was discovered here as early as 1859 by Warterman Bodey, but mining did not occur on a large scale for several years. By 1864 there were only twenty buildings in town, and by the early 1870s there had not been much more growth. In 1872, however, another vein was found, and the town was "discovered." With the creation of the Standard Consolidated Mining Company in 1877, miners flocked to Bodey. From 1876 to 1884 the town witnessed

Travertine Hot Springs.

boom growth, typical of so many western mining towns of the era. By 1879 the town's population was more than 10,000, and the spelling of its name was changed to Bodie to insure proper pronunciation. More than $30 million in gold and 1 million ounces of silver were extracted from the mines.

During its heyday, Bodie was known as one of the roughest towns in the country. Although the gunplay has undoubtedly been overplayed, Bodie's leading cause of death was bullets, and the death rate per capita was extremely high. A future resident, when learning that she was to live in the infamous town remarked in her diary, "Good-bye God, I'm going to Bodie."

Despite Bodie's decline in the late 1880s, several people hung around the town and Bodie became the first mining town to have electricity in 1893. Several fires ravaged the town over the years, but an amazing number of buildings remain to the present. Street outlines can be seen clearly, especially from a higher elevation, giving visitors an idea of just how big this town once was.

To reach Bodie travel south out of Bridgeport on US 395 for about 7 miles to signs for Bodie State Historic Park. Turn here and go east on California Highway 270 for about 12 miles to the park. The last few miles of the road are dirt, but most passenger cars will have no problem. The park is open year-round, 9 a.m. to 7 p.m. in summer and 9 a.m. to 4 p.m. the rest of the year. CA 270 is generally closed to motor vehicles during winter due to snowfall. The park can be reached by snowmobile, skis, or snowshoes during winter. Contact the Mono County Sheriff's office in Bridgeport for road and weather conditions before making the trip. For further information contact Bodie State Historic Park at (619) 647-6445.

59

Buckeye Hot Springs

General description: Two hot springs sources feeding two soaking pools adjacent to a clear stream on the eastern slope of the Sierras. Both pools offer excellent bathing opportunities.
Location: Eastern California, 10 miles northwest of Bridgeport.
Primitive/developed: Primitive, except for damming of the springs for bathing pools.
Best time of year: Spring, summer, or fall. There is substantial snow here in the winter, but you can ski to the spring relatively easily.
Restrictions: None.
Access: A high-clearance vehicle is best, although most sturdy passenger

vehicles with decent clearance will make it. During wet weather you will need four-wheel drive.

Water temperature: The sources are about 130 degrees F., but the water cools to around 100 degrees F. in the hillside pool. Temperatures in the creekside pools vary depending upon amount of creek water admitted.

Nearby attractions: Mono Lake, Yosemite National Park.

Services: None; gas, food, and lodging can be found 10 miles away in Bridgeport.

Camping: There is a Forest Service campground (Buckeye) less than a mile away from the spring.

Map: USGS Bridgeport, CA quadrangle (1:100,000 scale).

Finding the spring: At the north end of Bridgeport, turn left on Twin Lakes Road (before the last gas station in town). Travel about 7.1 miles to Doc and Al's Resort, then turn right on dirt Forest Road 017. Take this dirt road about 2.7 miles, following signs to Buckeye. After crossing Buckeye Creek (about 2.5 miles), stay straight and look for a large, flat area on your right. Park here. The springs are about 100 yards downstream from this parking area. Buckeye Campground is down a dirt road to the left after crossing the bridge.

Buckeye Hot Springs

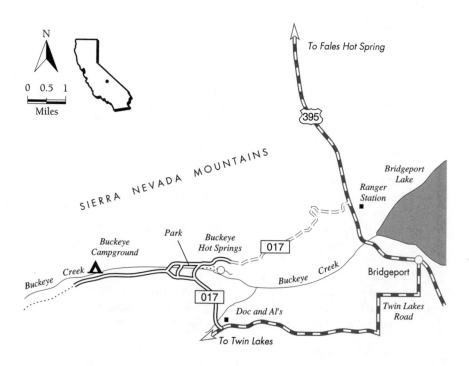

Buckeye Hot Springs.

An alternate route is to travel north out of Bridgeport for about 5 miles on US 395 to the ranger station, then turn onto a dirt road to the left (west). A Forest Service sign at the road will indicate Buckeye Campground. Travel on this one-lane, poor dirt road for about 5 miles to Buckeye Creek, where you can park in a wide area above the creek itself. Walk down the steep trail to the spring at the edge of the creek. The other pool will be slightly upstream and uphill. This route is more difficult, and can be impassable in wet weather. Since the road is one lane in places, take it slow and watch for oncoming vehicles.

The hot springs: The two main sources at Buckeye Hot Springs emerge from the side of the hill and cool rapidly at they flow downhill. In cold weather the hot springs will be easy to spot with all the steam. In warmer weather look for color changes on the side of the hill, where algae is growing. One of the sources flows into a 7- by 3-foot pool that maintains a temperature of about 100 degrees F. The other source is larger and flows into the creek where it has been dammed up with rocks, forming several pools. Each of these pools differs slightly in temperature, ranging from 110 to 95 degrees F. The temperature will vary depending upon the amount of creek water flowing into the pools. The largest pool is under the overhang created by the hot springs water, and offers a cavelike setting. The water coming off the overhang also produces a small waterfall.

This is a fantastic hot spring, adjacent to a clear running stream stocked with rainbow and brown trout. The water is a little hot in places at Buckeye, so use caution. Also be careful coming down to the creekside pools, since the ground is quite slippery. These are popular hot springs, so you can count on sharing them with others on summer weekends. If you choose to visit in the snowy part of winter, you should have them to yourself.

60

Dechambeau Hot Springs

General description: A series of high-temperature hot springs feeding several ponds at a bird sanctuary near Mono Lake. Bathing opportunities are limited, but there is a lot of wildlife and several other, bathable springs in the vicinity.

Location: Eastern California, about 15 miles northeast of Lee Vining.

Primitive/developed: Primitive, although a large well has been dug and several other changes made to promote the bird sanctuary.

Dechambeau Hot Springs.

Dechambeau Hot Springs

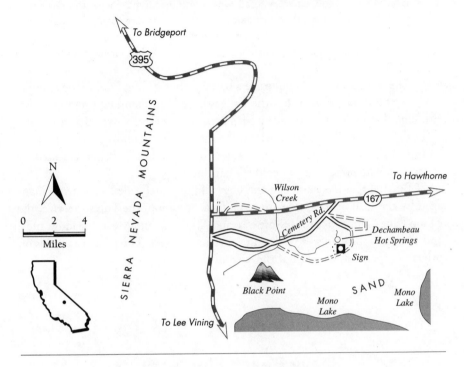

Best time of year: Year-round, though the road to the springs may be difficult in wet weather.

Restrictions: The springs are within a bird sanctuary run by the State of California, so all posted rules must be obeyed. There is also substantial private property in the area, which should be respected.

Access: Most passenger vehicles can access the springs. There are some slightly sandy spots in the road, but you won't need four-wheel drive.

Water temperature: Varies depending upon source; most average 130 degrees F. Several pools are slightly cooler but still too hot to bathe in.

Nearby attractions: Mono Lake, Yosemite National Park.

Services: None; gas, food, and lodging can be found 7 miles away in Lee Vining.

Camping: There do not appear to be any restrictions against camping near the springs, but you can't drive up to them and much of the immediate area is private property. It's better to camp at any of several developed and undeveloped campgrounds in the vicinity. Contact the Mono Lake Visitor Center and the Lee Vining Ranger Station for campsites in the area.

Map: USGS Bridgeport, CA-NV quadrangle (1:100,000 scale).

Finding the springs: From Lee Vining travel north on U.S. Highway 395 for 8 miles to U.S. Highway 167, where you turn right (east). Take US 167 about 4.3 miles to Cemetery Road, where you turn right. Follow this dirt road for a mile or so, then turn left again on a lesser dirt road. Continue for another 0.5 mile until you see the sign for the bird sanctuary. Park at the sign and walk the few hundred yards to the several hot springs sources.

The hot springs: Too hot to be a bathable hot spring, Dechambeau offers ample scenery. The hot springs themselves have been dammed up in the past, although the pools have not survived. The springs were discovered accidentally while drilling for oil. The well itself still remains, fenced off to protect the public from its scalding water. The hot water feeds several ponds that are used by waterfowl. The ponds are too cold for bathing.

Be careful at Dechambeau and obey all the posted rules. The area is managed by the California Department of Transportation, the Forest Service, the Mono Lake Committee to Restore Seasonal Wetlands and Moist Meadowlands, and Ducks Unlimited as a wetland restoration project. The nearby ranch is on private property, as is much of the surrounding land.

61

Navy Beach Hot Spring

General description: A deep pond formed by a single hot spring on the shores of Mono Lake. Once open to bathing, the spring has been shut down by the State of California, which claims that bacteria levels have risen.

Location: Eastern California, 10 miles from Lee Vining.

Primitive/developed: Primitive.

Best time of year: Year-round. The road to the springs may be impassable in wet weather.

Restrictions: This is a state park and at press time bathing is not allowed. Check-in with the Mono Lake Visitor Center south of Lee Vining for current regulations.

Access: Any vehicle. Although the dirt road has some sandy spots, as long as you stay on the road you should have no problem.

Water temperature: About 100 degrees F. in the pond.

Nearby attractions: Mono Lake, Yosemite National Park.

Services: None; the nearest gasoline, food, and lodging can be found in Lee Vining, 10 miles away.

Camping: Camping is not allowed. There are several state campgrounds

Navy Beach Hot Spring

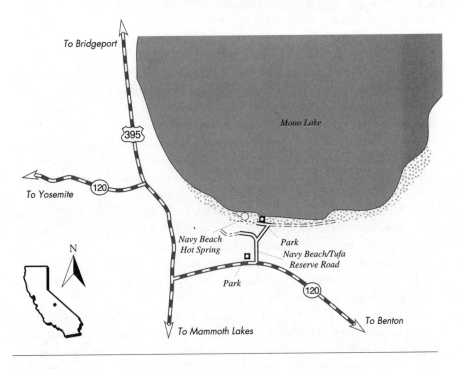

nearby, however. Check in with the Mono Lake Visitor Center or the Lee Vining Ranger Station.

Map: California State Highway map.

Finding the spring: From Lee Vining, travel south on U.S. Highway 395 for about 5 miles to California Highway 120, and turn left (east). Take CA 120 about 4 miles to a state park sign for the Tufa Reserve. Turn left on this dirt road, following the signs to Navy Beach. You'll reach the parking area in about 0.5 mile. A 0.25-mile trail leads from the west side of the parking area to the spring.

The hot spring: Navy Beach Hot Spring is an excellent pond for bathing—unfortunately, you are no longer allowed to use it in such a way. About 4 feet deep, the spring is about 100 degrees F. A few hundred yards from the shore of Mono Lake, it offers much to make up for the lack of bathing. Fabulous scenery, interesting geology, and abundant birdlife will greet you at Navy Beach.

Mono Lake: Encompassed by a 116,000-acre National Scenic Area, Mono Lake is a beautiful and multifaceted natural area. The youngest mountain range in California, the volcanic Mono Craters south of the lake erupted as recently as 600 years ago. Several of the volcanoes in the Mono Lake region are obsidian domes. Obsidian is a particularly glassy type of lava, black in color, and was a favorite material for tools among Native Americans. Picnic areas abound in the obsidian domes area, south of the lake, west and east of U.S. Highway 395.

The volcanic activity of the area is also evidenced by the many hot springs in the vicinity, including the two described above. Other hot springs can be found in the lake area, the most dramatic of which lies on Pahoha Island in the middle of the lake. This extremely hot spring was at one time used as a resort, but it has long since been abandoned, its buildings and baths in ruin. Some of the most remarkable features of the lake are its tufa towers, formed when the lake level was higher and calcium carbonate was precipitated from the springs, eventually forming these sometimes large outcrops.

Mono Lake itself is more than 700,000 years old. With no natural outlet, the waters in the lake are too salty to support fish populations. Brine shrimp live in the waters, however, providing abundant food for the many birds in the area. Several types of birds and waterfowl come to Mono Lake every year to nest and feed on shrimp and flies. The lake's many islands provide secure havens from predators for these migratory birds.

There are ample back roads to explore in this region, but close to the lake many of these roads are too sandy. Winter weather can be treacherous in the region. The best times to visit are summer, early fall, and late spring. An excellent visitors center was recently constructed north of Lee Vining, a must first stop. For further information contact the center at (619) 647-3000.

Mono Mills: Immediately off California Highway 120 past the turnoff for Navy Beach (20 miles from U.S. Highway 395) lie the remains of a large lumber mill used between 1876 and 1916. Wood from the surrounding mountains was cut at this mill for use in the mining town of Bodie. Wood was such a necessity in the mines that a narrow-gauge railway was constructed from Bodie all the way to this mill. Little is left of the Bodie & Benton Railroad today, although parts of the right-of-way can be seen in places. Some of the remains of the mill itself, and the camp where the workers lived, can still be seen.

62

Hot Creek

(See map on page 171.)

General description: A series of hot springs feeding a cold water creek in a national forest. The hot springs vary widely in temperature, but a few warm spots at this popular spot allow perfect mixing of water.

Location: Eastern California, 9 miles southeast of Mammoth Lakes.

Primitive/developed: The hot springs in the creek have not been developed, but dressing rooms, toilets, and a parking lot have been constructed nearby.

Best time of year: Spring, summer, or fall. The road to the springs may be closed in winter.

Restrictions: Hot Creek is open during daylight hours only. Obey all signs.

Access: Standard passenger vehicles should have no problem on the graded dirt road.

Water temperature: Varies depending upon source. Some of the springs

Hot Creek (from parking lot).

are extremely hot (130+ degrees F.), while other sources are cooler. The few bathable spots also vary in temperature.

Nearby attractions: Mammoth Lakes, Long Valley Hot Springs.

Services: None; gasoline, food, and lodging can be found 9 miles away in Mammoth Lakes.

Camping: No camping allowed. There are several Forest Service campgrounds in the area, and plenty of public land for undeveloped camping nearby.

Map: USGS Benton Range, CA-NV quadrangle (1:100,000 scale).

Finding the springs: From the junction of U.S. Highway 395 and California Highway 203 outside Mammoth Lakes, travel south on US 395 for about 3 miles. Turn left (east) on Hot Creek Road. Take this paved road for 0.8 mile to the sign for Hot Creek Geothermal Area, and turn right. Go another 3 miles on this paved, and then graded dirt, road to the parking area for Hot Creek. The hot springs are downhill in the creek along a steep, paved path.

The hot springs: A popular place for those visiting the Mammoth Lakes area, Hot Creek can be quite busy on weekends, particularly in summer. Although the road may be closed during winter, you can ski into the springs if you are so inclined. Most of the springs feeding the cold creek are extremely hot, which you can see by the vast amount of steam produced. In the main bathing area there are several springs bubbling up on the creek bottom. These also are quite hot, but mixed with cold water they can make an exhilarating bath. Be extremely careful here, since most of the springs are boiling temperature at the source and will scald you. Bathe only in the main beach area, and take caution. Hot Creek is not the place for seclusion, but it is worth an hour or two for a bath.

LONG VALLEY

There probably are more hot springs in Long Valley than in any other area described in this book. Many of these natural springs have been channeled, dammed, or diverted into soaking pools. Although not well known a few years ago, the area has become quite popular recently. But you should still be able to find a nice pond or tub for a great soak, always in a majestic setting.

Roads to the springs in Long Valley vary. The main access road east of U.S. Highway 395, Benton Crossing Road, is paved, and another road, FR 2507, is graded dirt. The roads leading from these two roads are unimproved dirt surfaces, however, and sandy in places. During wet weather, these roads become treacherous and should not be attempted.

Much of the land in this area is owned by the Los Angeles Department of Water and Power (LADWP), which generally allows daytime use. Some of the springs are on public land and have few or no restrictions against camping. LADWP land is marked with large white signs. Obey these signs so public access won't be denied in the future.

Hot Creek, The Hot Tub, Shepherd Hot Spring, Crab Cooker, Crowley (Wild Willy's) Hot Spring, Hilltop (Pulkey's Pool) Hot Spring, Little Hot Creek

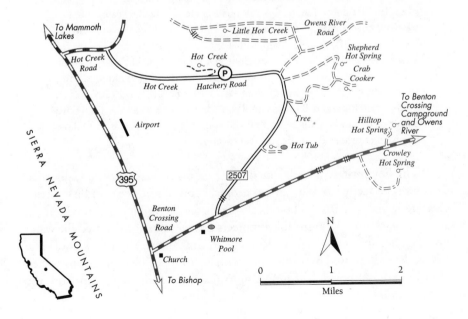

63

The Hot Tub

General description: A large bathtub-sized pool fed by a natural hot spring in the Eastern Sierra. The tub is built of rocks and cement, and water is piped into it from the spring, a short distance away. One of the best bathing spots in the state.

Location: Eastern California, 11 miles southeast of Mammoth Lakes.

Primitive/developed: Primitive, except for the hot tub and the piping of water into it.

Best time of year: Year-round. The road is best avoided during the occasional winter snowfall, when it can get muddy.

Restrictions: None.

Access: Any vehicle can make the short drive on a well-maintained, graded dirt road.

Water temperature: The temperature at the source is about 120 degrees F., but the tub is closer to 100 degrees F., varying slightly.

Nearby attractions: Mammoth Lakes, Hot Creek.

Services: None, but gas, food, and lodging can be found 11 miles away in Mammoth Lakes.

Camping: Camping is allowed at the spring, although frequently someone is already there. There are several Forest Service campgrounds in the area and plenty of public land for undeveloped camping nearby.

Map: USGS Benton Range, CA-NV quadrangle (1:100,000 scale).

Finding the spring: From the junction of U.S. Highway 395 and California Highway 203 outside Mammoth Lakes, travel south on US 395 for about 9 miles. Turn left (east) on Benton Crossing Road at a large, green church. Take this paved road for about 1.2 miles (passing Whitmore Pool) to the first graded dirt road on your left. This is Forest Road 2S07. Travel on this road for about 1.1 miles until you come up to a small hill. Turn onto a faint dirt road on your right. You will soon see the source. If you follow the road another 100 yards you will reach the tub.

The hot springs: This is one of the best places for a soak in California. The tub is perfectly sized for several people, about 2 feet deep, and has a temperature in the low 100s. The tub also faces the Sierra Nevada, providing an awesome backdrop. Resourceful volunteers several years ago diverted the water from the hot spring through a PVC pipe to this concrete and rock pool. The tub has been improved over the years, with a patio-like area being constructed most recently. Although it is only a short distance off the main dirt road, the

Hot Tub is not visible from the road, providing a good deal of privacy. The spring is one of the most popular in the area, however, and you can expect to find others there before you. Your best chance for seclusion is during the week in winter or fall. Please help to keep the area pristine by packing out all your trash and staying on established roads.

64

Shepherd Hot Spring

(See map on page 171.)

General description: Another fantastic tub created by the diversion of hot spring water into a small concrete pool. This spring is similar to others in the area, but requires driving on a rougher road.

Location: Eastern California, 12 miles southeast of Mammoth Lakes.

Primitive/developed: Primitive, except for the hot pool and the piping of water into it.

Best time of year: Spring, summer, or fall. The road may be quite difficult during wet weather and impassable in snow.

Restrictions: The land at the tub itself is owned by the LADWP, and their rules must be obeyed.

Access: A high-clearance vehicle is best, although all kinds of passenger vehicles can make it. Avoid this spring if the road is wet unless you have four-wheel drive.

Water temperature: The temperature at the source itself is about 115 degrees F. and cools to about 110 degrees F. in the tub. The water can get quite hot if you sit in it awhile. You can lower the temperature by diverting water out of the tub and waiting for it to cool.

Nearby attractions: Mammoth Lakes, Hot Creek.

Services: None, but gas, food, and lodging can be found 12 miles away in Mammoth Lakes.

Camping: Camping is permitted on public land a few hundred yards west of the spring. Do not camp at Shepherd Hot Spring itself. There are also several Forest Service campgrounds in the area and a semi-developed campground at Benton Crossing, a few miles east on Owens River Road.

Map: USGS Benton Range, CA-NV quadrangle (1:100,000 scale).

Finding the spring: From the junction of U.S. Highway 395 and California Highway 203 outside Mammoth Lakes, travel south on US 395 for about 9 miles. Turn left (east) on Benton Crossing Road at a large, green church. Take this paved road for about 1 mile (past Whitmore Pool) to the

Shepherd Hot Spring.

first graded, dirt road on your left. This is Forest Road 2SO7. Travel on this road for about 2 miles, passing the road to the Hot Tub (Spring 63), and turn right on a smaller dirt road on your right a few yards before a lone tree. Continue on this lesser-maintained road for about 0.8 mile. The road will curve around a boggy area, then fork. Stay to the left and drive the last few yards to the tub, on your right. To get to the Crab Cooker (Spring 65), turn right at the fork and go downhill a few hundred yards. Stay on the road to avoid getting stuck in the boggy marsh. The road is sandy in a few places, but if you keep on the main part of the road you should have no problems.

The hot springs: This is another fantastic place to soak, although not quite as secluded as the Hot Tub. The water is also quite a bit hotter, so you cannot stay in as long. Sheepherders built this tub quite a few years ago by diverting hot spring water through a plastic pipe into a cement and rock tub. The tub is about 6 by 5 feet and 2 feet deep. It can be emptied by removing a drain plug at the end and diverting the water. People generally keep it clean by replacing the water and scrubbing the sides with a brush.

This spring has also been kept clean and free from trash—do your part to keep it that way. Although camping was allowed at one time, a few years ago the

LADWP posted signs forbidding it. There is plenty of public land to the west where camping is allowed. You can always camp there and walk to the tub.

65

Crab Cooker

(See map on page 171.)

General description: Another bathtub-sized pool fed by a natural hot spring in the Eastern Sierra. A little less popular than other tubs in the region, the Crab Cooker is another great place to soak.

Location: Eastern California, 12 miles southeast of Mammoth Lakes.

Primitive/developed: Primitive, except for construction of the hot tub and the piping of water into it.

Best time of year: Spring, summer, or fall. The road may be quite difficult during wet weather and impassable in snow.

Restrictions: The tub property itself is owned by the LADWP, and all posted rules must be obeyed.

Access: A high-clearance vehicle is best, although I've seen all kinds of passenger vehicles make it. Avoid this spring if the road is wet, unless you have four-wheel drive. The last few hundred yards to the spring can be difficult. Walk them if you are unsure whether your car can make it.

Water temperature: The source itself is extremely hot and has been covered over. The water cools substantially in the tub, averaging 105 degrees F.

Nearby attractions: Mammoth Lakes, Hot Creek.

Services: None; gas, food, and lodging can be found 12 miles away in Mammoth Lakes.

Camping: Camping is not allowed at the spring, but you can park a few hundred yards west and camp there. There are several Forest Service campgrounds in the area.

Map: USGS Benton Range, CA-NV quadrangle (1:100,000 scale).

Finding the spring: From the junction of U.S. Highway 395 and California Highway 203 outside Mammoth Lakes, travel south on US 395 for about 9 miles. Turn left (east) on Benton Crossing Road at a large, green church. Take this paved road for about a mile (past Whitmore Pool) to the first graded dirt road on your left. This is Forest Road 2S07. Travel on FR 2S07 for about 2 miles, passing the road to the Hot Tub (Spring 63), and turn right on a smaller dirt road on your right a few yards before a lone tree. Take this unmaintained road about 0.8 mile to where it curves around

Crab Cooker.

a boggy area, then forks. To get to the Crab Cooker, turn right at this fork
and go downhill a few hundred yards to a large grassy area. If you don't
think your car can make the last part of the drive, walk the short distance
to the spring. Stay on established roads, since there is a good chance that
you will get stuck in the boggy marsh if you don't.

The hot springs: The Crab Cooker is another nice place for a bath, similar to the Hot Tub and Shepherd Hot Springs. It is a little shallower than the
others, but big enough for several people. It also provides beautiful scenery.
Camping was once permitted at the tub, but is now prohibited. You can camp
a few hundred yards west, however. In some ways this regulation is better, since
you will generally not find a group of people camping at the spring and mo-
nopolizing it for their own use. Be sure to keep the area clean and free from
trash.

66

Crowley (Wild Willy's) Hot Spring

(See map on page 171.)

General description: A larger pond and smaller tub fed by a couple of hot spring sources in the scenic eastern Sierra. Although you must walk the last 100 yards to Crowley, it is still a popular spring and generally occupied.

Location: Eastern California, 14 miles southeast of Mammoth Lakes.

Primitive/developed: Primitive, except for construction of the pool and tub and the diversion of water into them.

Best time of year: Spring, summer, or fall. The road can be difficult or impassable in wet weather, particularly in snow.

Restrictions: You are not allowed to drive out to the spring itself, and camping is not permitted.

Access: Most passenger vehicles can make the 1.2-mile drive to the parking area. Do not try the road when it is wet or snow covered.

Water temperature: The source itself is about 115 degrees F. The pool is about 95 degrees F., and the tub is about 105 degrees F.

Nearby attractions: Mammoth Lakes, Hot Creek.

Services: None; gas, food, and lodging can be found 14 miles away in Mammoth Lakes.

Camping: Camping is not allowed at the spring itself. There is plenty of public land nearby for undeveloped camping. There are also several Forest Service campgrounds in the area.

Map: USGS Benton Range, CA-NV quadrangle (1:100,000 scale).

Finding the spring: From the junction of U.S. Highway 395 and California Highway 203 outside Mammoth Lakes, travel south on US 395 for about 9 miles. Turn left (east) on Benton Crossing Road at a large, green church. Travel on this paved road for about 3.1 miles, passing Forest Road 2SO7. As you cross a cattle guard, there is a small dirt road on your right; turn here. Follow this dirt road around the fenceline and downhill over 1.2 miles to a parking area. Walk the last few hundred yards to the spring and the pools. At all times, stay on the main road and you will not get stuck. When this soil gets wet it is extremely mucky.

The hot springs: Crowley has a nice, big pool complete with a wooden deck at its edge. The pool was built of concrete quite a few years ago and is about 9 feet by 12 feet, and 3 feet deep. The smaller tub is also enjoyable, with enough room for one or possibly two. The wood-lined tub is a few degrees

Crowley Hot Spring.

hotter than the pool. The area has been kept clean, particularly since cars were forbidden from driving right to the springs. As with most of the others, camping was once permitted at the spring itself but is no longer allowed. Again, there is plenty of public land nearby where camping is permitted. Just obey any signs you see and you should be fine.

67

Hilltop (Pulkey's Pool) Hot Spring

(See map on page 171.)

General description: A newer, smaller concrete tub fed by a hot spring source a few yards away. Atop a hill, this spring has a fantastic view of the surrounding countryside and the Sierra Nevada.

Location: Eastern California, 13 miles southeast of Mammoth Lakes.

Primitive/developed: Primitive, except for construction of the hot tub and the piping of water into it.

Best time of year: Year-round.

Restrictions: The property is owned by the LADWP, and camping is not allowed. Obey all signs.

Access: The spring is on a decent dirt road only 0.25 mile off a paved road. When it is dry most standard passenger vehicles can make the drive. When the ground is wet, however, you are much better off walking from the paved road. The soil here gets extremely mucky when wet, and you stand a good chance of getting hopelessly mired.

Water temperature: The source itself is about 115 degrees F., but cools to around 100 degrees F. in the tub. Tub temperature can be altered by diverting water out to cool.

Nearby attractions: Mammoth Lakes, Hot Creek.

Services: None; gas, food, and lodging can be found 11 miles away in Mammoth Lakes.

Camping: Camping is not allowed at the spring. There are several Forest Service campgrounds in the area and plenty of public land nearby where camping also is permitted.

Map: USGS Benton Range, CA-NV quadrangle (1:100,000 scale).

Finding the spring: From the junction of U.S. Highway 395 and California Highway 203 outside Mammoth Lakes, travel south on US 395 for about 9 miles. Turn left (east) on Benton Crossing Road at a large, green church. Travel on this paved road for about 3.4 miles (0.2 mile past the road to Crowley Hot Spring) to a dirt road on your left. Turn here and drive 0.25 mile to a parking area. Park here and walk the short distance uphill to the tub. If the ground is wet, do not drive on this dirt road, since it passes through a low spot where water collects. Pull off the paved road and walk the short distance instead.

The hot springs: Hilltop Hot Spring is a relatively new tub in the area, sometimes known as Pulkey's Pool. The tub is similar to others nearby, consisting of a concrete tub fed by hot spring water piped from a few yards away. This tub can also be cleaned by draining it and diverting the water out. About 6 feet by 4 feet and 2 feet deep, Hilltop makes a nice bath, big enough for several people. This spring is lesser known than others in the area, but it does get crowded on weekends, particularly in summer.

The spring is on land owned by the LADWP, so camping is not permitted. You can, however, find plenty of public land in the area—all the undeveloped space you could want. Since visitors cannot drive right to the tub, it has been kept in relatively good condition and free from trash. Help keep it this way.

68

Little Hot Creek

(See map on page 171.)

General description: A hotter, larger spring and tub removed a few miles from the other hot springs in the area. A great place for a hot soak, Little Hot Creek has a beautiful setting and fantastic views.
Location: Eastern California, 16 miles southeast of Mammoth Lakes.
Primitive/developed: Primitive, except for construction of the hot tub and the piping of water into it.
Best time of year: Spring, summer, or fall. Secondary roads can be difficult in wet weather and impassable in snow.
Restrictions: None.
Access: Most standard passenger vehicles should be able to make the drive without too much trouble when the road is dry. Avoid altogether when wet.
Water temperature: The source itself is about 150 degrees F., and cools to about 115 degrees F. by the time it reaches the tub. Since this is too hot, cool it off by diverting water for a while.
Nearby attractions: Mammoth Lakes, Hot Creek.
Services: None; gas, food, and lodging can be found 11 miles away in Mammoth Lakes.
Camping: The hot spring is on Forest Service land, and there do not appear to be any restrictions against camping. Do not camp adjacent to the spring itself, however. There are several developed Forest Service campgrounds in the area and plenty of public land nearby where camping also is permitted.
Map: USGS Benton Range, CA-NV quadrangle (1:100,000 scale).
Finding the spring: From the junction of U.S. Highway 395 and California Highway 203 outside Mammoth Lakes, travel south on US 395 for about 9 miles. Turn left (east) on Benton Crossing Road at a large, green

church. Take this paved road about 1 mile, passing Whitmore Pool, to the first graded, dirt road on your left. This is Forest Road 2SO7. Travel on FR 2SO7 for about 3.3 miles, passing roads to the Hot Tub, Shepherd Hot Springs, and the Crab Cooker, until you reach the Owens River Road. To the left is the road to Hot Creek; you continue to the right. Cross the creek and turn left at the next intersection, staying on Owens River Rd. Continue another 0.7 mile to Antelope Road, where you turn left. This road is not as well maintained as Owens River Rd., but should be fine as long as it's dry. Drive on Antelope Rd. about 2.5 miles to a cattle guard. Immediately past the cattle guard, turn right and go another 0.8 mile to the springs. You will need to walk through a cattle-proof gate to get to the tub itself.

The hot springs: The extremely hot water at Little Hot Creek is diverted from one of a cluster of hot springs through several yards of pipes into a concrete pool, where the water remains hot. A series of fences have been built around the spring to reduce cattle damage. The tub is about 8 feet by 9 feet and 2 feet deep. Be careful here, since the water is hot. Before getting in, feel the water temperature and divert the pipe from the tub to let the water cool. This tub is the least known spring in the area, but that does not guarantee seclusion. The road to the tub is longer than the others, but is passable to most vehicles when it is dry.

Unlike the other area springs, this tub is located on Forest Service land and does not appear to have any restrictions against camping. Do not camp immediately adjacent to the tub, however, and please pick up after yourself.

Owens Valley—Eastern Sierra, Southern Part

South of Long Valley lies the lower Owens Valley, with the communities of Bishop, Big Pine, Independence, and Lone Pine. This area is generally warmer than regions to the north, and less watered. The Owens River flows through the valley but is picked up by the Los Angeles Department of Water and Power (LADWP) canal. The river at one time flowed into now-dry Owens Lake and eventually disappeared into the desert, but the water now goes to the City of Los Angeles. Ample creeks drain the high Sierra from the west, flowing under U.S. Highway 395 and into the Owens River. Most of these creeks are stocked with various types of game fish and make excellent fishing spots. Campgrounds and picnic spots abound along U.S. Highway 395 between Bishop and Lone Pine. All services can be obtained in any of the four towns, although Bishop is by far the largest.

69

Keough Hot Ditch

General description: A group of pools of varying temperature formed in a creek of hot spring water. Located off U.S. Highway 395, the water forming these pools is from a source that supplies a bathhouse uphill.

Location: Eastern California, 8 miles south of Bishop.

Primitive/developed: Primitive, except for damming of some of the pools.

Best time of year: Year-round.

Restrictions: This is LADWP land, and is only open to the public during daytime.

Access: Any passenger vehicle can make the short drive off the highway. To go farther and access some of the pools, you will need some clearance.

Water temperature: The sources are quite hot, about 130 degrees F. at the top of the hill. The water cools as it flows downhill, and each pool is therefore cooler as you go down the incline. Temperatures range from 110 degrees F. on the hillside to 90 degrees F. on the other side of the road.

Keough Hot Springs/Ditch.

Keough Hot Ditch

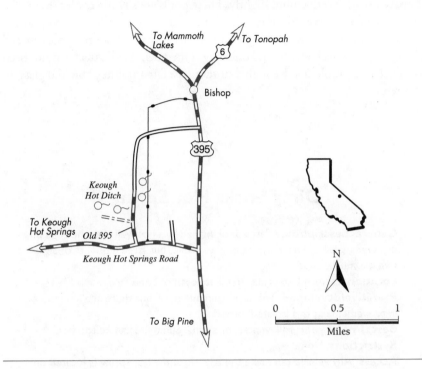

Nearby attractions: Lake Sabrina, Owens River, numerous fishing creeks.
Services: None, but all services can be found 8 miles away in Bishop.
Camping: Camping is not allowed. Seek out any of several Forest Service and private campgrounds in the area.
Map: USGS Bishop, CA quadrangle (1:100,000 scale).
Finding the spring: From Bishop, travel south on U.S. Highway 395 for about 7 miles to Keough Hot Springs Road—there will be a yellow highway sign—and turn right. Take this paved road for about 0.6 mile to an old paved road near a powerline, where you turn right again. Drive on this road (old US 395) for 0.25 mile, where you will see the springs on your left up a smaller road. There are also three groups of springs on your right. Take your pick of the many pools here.

The hot springs: Keough Hot Springs Resort, which closed recently, is up the road from Keough Hot Ditch. It used to be a popular warm swimming pool. Keough Hot Ditch is formed from several sources uphill, which flow down a small creek that has been dammed in places for bathing opportunities. The pools are fairly large and decrease in temperature as you go downhill. The water is generally clear and inviting. A second collection of pools is across the old paved road and downhill slightly. These pools are slightly cooler (high 90s) but are also fairly large. Although this is a popular place, with so many pools to choose from you should be able to find one to yourself. If all the pools are full when you arrive, wait awhile and one may come open. So far, trash has not been too much of a problem at Keough, but there is a fair amount of broken glass, so be careful.

70

Dirty Socks Hot Spring

General description: A large pool formed by a hot well near the edge of dry Owens Lake. The warm pool is bathable, but large amounts of algae give it a murky appearance.

Location: Eastern California, 26 miles south of Lone Pine.

Primitive/developed: This is a manmade pool, but there are few other improvements at this isolated location.

Best time of year: Fall, winter, or spring. Summers can be too hot.

Restrictions: None.

Access: Any vehicle can make the trip, since the hot spring is located on the end of a paved road.

Water temperature: About 90 degrees F. in the center of the pool, and cooler in other places.

Nearby attractions: Death Valley, the ghost towns of Darwin and Keeler.

Services: None, but gas, food, and lodging can be found 26 miles away in Lone Pine. There are a few small hotels in Olancha, 5 miles away.

Camping: There do not appear to be any restrictions against camping at Dirty Socks.

Map: USGS Darwin Hills, CA quadrangle (1:100,000 scale).

Finding the spring: From Lone Pine travel south on U.S. Highway 395 and turn left (east) on California Highway 190, which leads toward Death Valley. Go about 5 miles to an unmarked paved road on the left. Follow this road about 0.25 mile to the pond at the end of the road.

The hot springs: Dirty Socks Hot Spring is a large (30- by 30- foot) pool of warm water on the edge of a dry lake in arid Owens Valley. The pool is 4 to 5 feet deep, and about 90 degrees F. The water has algae growing in it, which won't hurt you but gives the pool an unappealing appearance. Although it is rather well known, the spring does not receive many visitors due to its murky look.

Dirty Socks was apparently discovered accidentally when the Southern Pacific Railroad was drilling wells in the area and hit hot water. An enterprising individual later bought the property, and built a pool and resort at the spring. The resort failed rather quickly, and all that remains today is the large pool. The name Dirty Socks probably came from the sulfurous smell given off by the water.

Owens Valley: Prior to the diversion of water out of the Owens River by Los Angeles in the early 1900s, Owens Lake was actually full of water. Named in the 1850s by John Charles Frémont for a member of his third expedition, the lake was 15 miles long, 9 miles wide, and 50 feet deep in 1891.

As hard as it is to imagine, steamboats traversed Owens Lake at one time. During the 1860s, at the height of production of the mines at Cerro Gordo, in the mountains to the east, ore was hauled over the mountains and down to Swansea, on the lake's northeast shore. From Swansea it was loaded on the steamship *Bessie Brady*, steamed across the lake, and unloaded at Cartago, on the southwest shore. This 85-foot steamboat saved freighters more than 50 miles

Dirty Socks Hot Spring

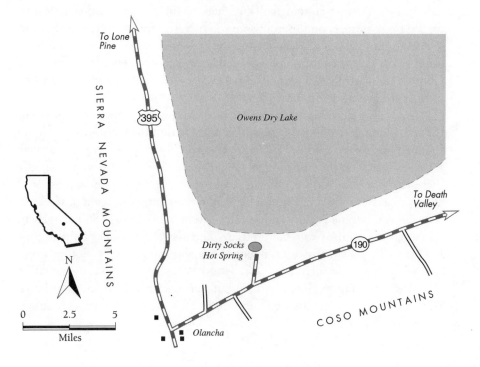

Dirty Socks Hot Spring.

and four days' travel around the lake. Fuel, wood, and charcoal was in turn carried from Swansea on the steamship *Molly Stevens* for use in the smelters on the north shore. From Cartago the ore was freighted to Los Angeles, and from there to San Francisco for refining. The massive amount of ore from the Cerro Gordo mines (worth $15 million) is believed to have been an impetus for the growth of Los Angeles in the 1870s.

Following a decline in mining at Cerro Gordo, a rejuvenation occurred in the late 1870s. In conjunction with this rejuvenation the Carson & Colorado Railroad was constructed in 1883 from Carson City to its terminus at the new town of Keeler, on the east shore of Owens Lake. The mines declined rapidly thereafter, however, and the railroad saw little use. Today the line is long since abandoned, but the depot can still be seen in the semi-ghost town of Keeler.

Settlers began to stake claims in the Owens Valley in the 1860s, largely to take advantage of the Cerro Gordo trade. The first Owens Valley farmers grew hay for feeding the many teams plying the region and a variety of other crops, supplying miners throughout the 1860s and 1870s. Sheep and cattle ranching also prospered in the region. Nearby mining areas such as Darwin, Candelaria, Ballarat, and Panamint City were supplied by these farms and ranches in subsequent decades.

In 1904 the growing city of Los Angeles sought additional water, finding it in the Owens River. By 1907 the city had built an aqueduct (portions of which can still be seen today) to carry the water to Los Angeles, more than 250 miles away. As the city grew, more water was drawn out of the valley. Local ranchers and farmers fought for their water, with numerous skirmishes, through the 1920s. Los Angeles was the eventual victor, however, buying up enough property to acquire control of the valley's resources. The once fertile Owens Valley farms and ranches soon dried up, leaving only a handful of settlers able to make a living off the land.

SALINE VALLEY

A trip to one of the most isolated, unpopulated, and forbidding regions in California, the Saline Valley, is an expedition. Northwest of Death Valley National Park, Saline is in many ways far more treacherous. The only roads leading into and out of the valley are poor, unimproved dirt surfaces, winding long distances from the nearest paved highway. Portions of these roads are sandy, steep, and lined with large rocks. Any vehicle attempting to enter the region should have high clearance (four-wheel drive is recommended) and be in good working order. For those willing to take the long trek into the valley, there are several hot springs waiting as a reward.

Contact the Bureau of Land Management in Ridgecrest and Death Valley National Park for up-to-date regulations, road conditions, and restrictions. Take all precautions before you go. Notify someone of your trip and when you plan to return. Bring more food and water than you could possibly use, along with tools, camping equipment, and other supplies listed in the introduction to this book.

71

Saline Valley Hot Springs

General description: An extremely isolated series of hot springs in a low desert environment. Despite their isolation, the springs are visited heavily and groups of people stay for extended periods. Several concrete tubs have been constructed at the three sets of springs.
Location: Eastern California, 105 miles northeast of Lone Pine.
Primitive/developed: These hot springs are natural, but there have been

Saline Valley Hot Springs

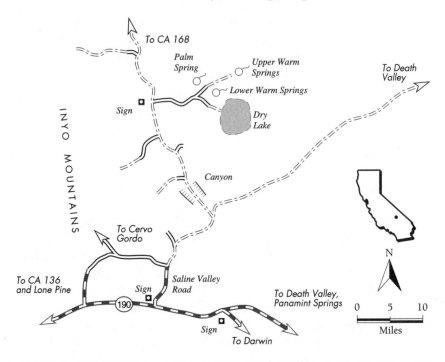

substantial improvements, including construction of concrete tubs, a shower, an outhouse, and a camp. The upper hot springs are primitive.

Best time of year: Fall, winter, or spring. Summers are extremely hot.

Restrictions: None.

Access: This is a difficult road requiring a sturdy vehicle in sound condition. High clearance is necessary, and you may need four-wheel drive if the road has been washed out. Do not attempt this drive if the roads are wet or if rain is approaching.

Water temperature: Varies depending upon the hot spring. Most of the concrete tubs are around 100 degrees F.

Nearby attractions: Death Valley National Park, the ghost towns of Darwin and Cerro Gordo.

Services: None, but all services can be found 105 miles away in Lone Pine.

Camping: Camping is permitted for up to 30 days, and volunteers have made a comfortable camp that includes dish basins, makeshift showers, plenty of shade, couches, and a shower.

Maps: Death Valley National Park map; USGS Darwin Hills, CA quadrangle (1:100,000 scale).

Saline Valley Hot Springs.

Finding the springs: From Lone Pine, travel south on U.S. Highway 395 to California Highway 136 and turn left (east) toward Death Valley. Go 18 miles to where CA 136 intersects with California Highway 190, and stay left following CA 190. Go another 17 miles to a sign for Saline Valley, and turn left. Continue on this road, staying right at the first fork, then left at the next fork, which leads you down a steep canyon. After about 44 miles you will turn right at another dirt road with either a sign or a painted rock. Travel on this road for about 10 miles, staying left at another fork, eventually reaching a palm tree where the first set of hot springs (Lower Warm Springs) are located. The second set, Palm Springs, are another mile up the same road. Undeveloped Upper Warm Springs are another 5 miles of treacherous road beyond this.

The hot springs: On Bureau of Land Management land, this group of hot springs consists of Lower Warm Springs, Palm Springs—where an extensive camp has been built, with several concrete soaking pools—and a third cluster of springs (Upper Warm Springs) that consists only of several natural pools. The two lower springs are visited frequently during non-summer months, with many people staying days, weeks, and even months at a time. The springs are well maintained by these volunteers, and you get a real sense of cooperation and decency among those who so painstakingly care for the area. The camp has the convenience of a developed campground but maintains a sense of isolation. If you want seclusion, your best bet is to come during the week and make the extra 5-mile trip to the upper springs.

Be forewarned that many visitors to Saline Valley Hot Springs prefer to go without clothes. Many of these people go nude in the pools and just about everywhere else, too.

Plan ahead before making this trip. Pack plenty of extra water and food (more than you think you will need), a complete tool kit, a shovel, a spare tire, and a working car jack. Check your car thoroughly before you go, and let someone know where you are going and when you are coming back. This is an enjoyable hot spring to visit, but the trip can be dangerous if you are not prepared.

POINT SUR AND LOS PADRES NATIONAL FOREST

In marked contrast to Saline Valley, Big Sur is a small community in the lushly vegetated Pacific Coastal strip, immediately below a range of mountains. The mountains are largely managed by Los Padres National Forest. Although portions of the range are well watered and lush in vegetation, a large percentage of the country is dry scrub with few trees. The Coast Range mountains are rugged, with steep sides and canyons cut by several year-round creeks. To reach the only natural hot spring described in this section you must make a long hike of 10 miles. But there are other hot springs in the region, including those at the Esalen Institute near the town of Big Sur, which can be utilized by guests; call (408) 667-3047. Another set of hot springs lies to the north, in the rugged mountains near Carmel Valley. Tassajara Springs is primarily a Buddhist meditation center, but can be used by the public if you call ahead, (415) 431-3771.

72

Sykes Hot Spring

General description: A cluster of natural hot spring pools at a popular backpacking campground in the forested Coast Range. Accessible only by foot on a 10-mile trail, this spring is nevertheless popular and frequently visited.

Location: Western California, 10 miles east of Big Sur and 36 miles southeast of Monterey.

Primitive/developed: Primitive.

Best time of year: Year-round.

Restrictions: The spring is in Los Padres National Forest, and you must obtain a wilderness permit ahead of time.

Access: Only by foot, and because of the distance you will need to carry a backpack and stay overnight.

Water temperature: About 100 degrees F. in the largest pool, slightly cooler in the smaller.

Nearby attractions: Pacific Coast, Monterey.

Services: None, but all services can be found 36 miles away in Monterey. Limited services in the small town of Big Sur, near the trailhead.

Camping: Backpack camping is permitted, but you must obtain a wilderness permit prior to your trip.

Sykes Hot Spring

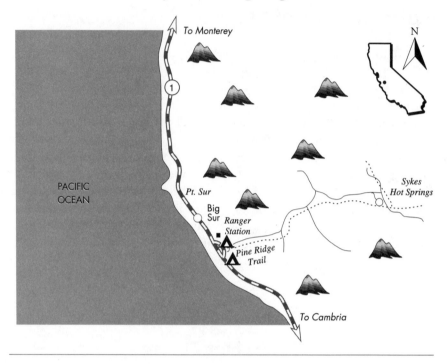

Maps: Los Padres National Forest Map; USGS Point Sur, CA quadrangle (1:100,000 scale).

Finding the spring: From Monterey, travel south on California Highway 1 for about 30 miles to the town of Big Sur. Continue a short distance out of town to Pfeiffer Big Sur State Park, where there is a parking lot and ranger station. Check in with this ranger station to obtain maps and trail information. The trail you'll want to take is the Pine Ridge Trail, and its trailhead is on the east side of the parking lot.

The 10-mile hike is difficult for the first few miles as you climb through scrub vegetation with no shade. The trail eventually levels out in the forest and becomes quite nice. The trail will eventually reach a substantial creek, which you will follow to the left for the last mile to the springs, on its bank.

The hot spring: Sykes Hot Spring is a delightful natural spring adjacent to a rushing creek. The largest pool is sheltered on one side by a large boulder, and by deadfall on the other. The water maintains a temperature of 100 degrees F., just the thing after a 10-mile hike. The long hike does not guarantee you seclusion or having the spring to yourself. There will generally be other people camping at the spring, particularly on summer weekends. If you prefer solitude, try going midweek, and if people are still there, wait till they vacate the spring to enjoy it. You will need to pack all your necessities to this location, since it is far too far to do the round-trip in a day. Be sure to obey all backcountry rules and etiquette by packing out all your trash, not dumping waste of any kind in the creek, and leaving no trace. For wilderness permits, maps, and further guidelines, contact the ranger station at (408) 667-2423.

SOUTHERN CALIFORNIA

Boasting California's largest concentration of people, the southern half of California still offers many opportunities for getting away from it all. Southern California includes the Mojave Desert in its eastern portion. The largest concentration of people lies to the west, along the coast from the Transverse Ranges north of Santa Barbara to San Diego and the international border with Mexico. Although it is not a geothermally active region, there are a few hot springs to be enjoyed here, in a variety of settings. In the desert, remote hot springs in the mountains and a funky resort near Death Valley await your visit. Closer to the city, hot springs may be found immediately off major highways or by driving a few hours off the main roads. Most visits to springs in this region can be combined with trips to other points of interest or to hot springs described elsewhere in this book.

LAKE ISABELLA AND THE KERN RIVER

Lake Isabella lies in the southern Sierra Nevada, a few hours from the farming community of Bakersfield. The lake was created from the damming of the Kern River in the 1950s to provide flood control, irrigation, and recreational opportunities. The lake has allowed the San Joaquin Valley to develop as one of the most agriculturally productive regions in the nation. The lake lies in a small valley bordered on all sides by high mountains. The lake is also lined with countless boat ramps, picnic spots, campgrounds, and marinas, and is a popular place for fishing, boating, and water-skiing during summer.

The main thoroughfare through the area is California Highway 178, running from Bakersfield in the west to California Highway 14 and U.S. Highway 395 in the east. CA 178 east of Lake Isabella crosses the Sierras at Walker Pass, discovered by mountain man Joseph Reddeford Walker in 1834. Other paved roads lead the traveler from the lake to high country in Sequoia National Forest to the north. The community of Lake Isabella is the largest in the area, offering all services. Kernville, at the north end of the lake, and Weldon on the east, also provide traveler services, including gas, food, and lodging.

Although only four hot springs are profiled here, there are several other natural hot springs in the region, most of which are privately owned and inaccessible to the public. Each of the hot springs described are relatively easy to reach since they are immediately off paved roads. Do not expect seclusion. As with so many other hot springs described in this book, several in this region were once resorts. All that remains today are concrete tubs and traces of the old buildings.

73

Remington Hot Spring

(See map on page 196.)

General description: Two cement soaking pools fed by natural hot spring water along the Kern River. Near Lake Isabella and a campground, this hot spring has many visitors but is worth a stop for a soak.

Location: Central California, 7.5 miles west of Lake Isabella.

Primitive/developed: Primitive, except for cement tubs.

Best time of year: Year-round. Summer can be hot.

Restrictions: None. Considered an environmentally fragile area. May be closed to public use in the future.

Access: Any vehicle can make the trip. You must hike a steep 300 yards to get to the tubs.

Water temperature: About 104 degrees F. at the source and 102 degrees F. in the tub.

Nearby attractions: Lake Isabella, Kern River Canyon.

Services: None; gas, food, and lodging can be found 6 miles away in Lake Isabella.

Camping: Camping is not permitted at the parking area above the spring, and there is no room to camp at the spring itself. There is a Forest Service campground (Hobo) 1.5 miles east.

Map: USGS Lake Isabella, CA quadrangle (1:100,000 scale).

Finding the spring: From Lake Isabella townsite, travel south on Lake Isabella Road to Kern River Canyon Road on the right, and drive to Hobo Campground (see Spring 75). Instead of pulling into the campground, continue west on Kern River Canyon Road (old California Highway 178) for about 1.5 miles to a turnout on the right, a broad parking area at the edge

Remington Hot Spring, California, upper pool.

of the canyon. This pullout is the second pullout you will pass, both with telephone poles in the middle of them. Park here and find a faint trail down the steep hillside. Walk about 300 yards or 0.25 mile to the river's edge, where there are two concrete and rock pools adjacent to one another. From the riverside pools there is another smaller pool uphill less than 50 yards. This third pool is a little more difficult to find, although with a little searching it shouldn't take long.

The hot springs: Remington Hot Spring is yet another abandoned hot spring resort. Remains of the resort can be seen in several places, although the hot spring itself has since been diverted into concrete and rock pools. Remington is in a beautiful setting on the banks of the rushing Kern River. The two pools along the river are 6 feet by 2 feet, and 2 to 3 feet deep. Temperatures in the pools range from 95 to 105 degrees F. The pools are high enough above the river to prevent their inundation, although in rare floods this may not be the case. The higher pool is smaller, and well enough away from the river to prevent its inundation.

Remington is another well-known hot spring where privacy and seclusion are rare. Occasionally you can be the only one at the hot spring, but this is usually on weekdays during the off season (winter). Because this spring is off the beaten track, many people choose to bathe in the nude. Be sure to pack out all trash when visiting the spring and be careful when heading down the steep trail to the spring. There is also an abundance of poison oak in the area, so don't venture off into the bushes. For more information, contact Sequoia National Forest at (209) 784-1500.

74

Miracle Hot Spring

General description: Several cement soaking pools fed by natural spring water along the Kern River. A one-time resort, Miracle Hot Spring offers several different hand-built pools. Immediately adjacent to a campground, the spring is heavily visited.

Location: Central California, 6 miles west of Lake Isabella.

Primitive/developed: Primitive, except for the cement tubs.

Best time of year: Year-round. Summer can be hot.

Restrictions: "Friends of the Hot Springs" collects $5 per vehicle to support the hot spring, and the group also patrols the spring.

Remington Hot Spring, Miracle Hot Spring

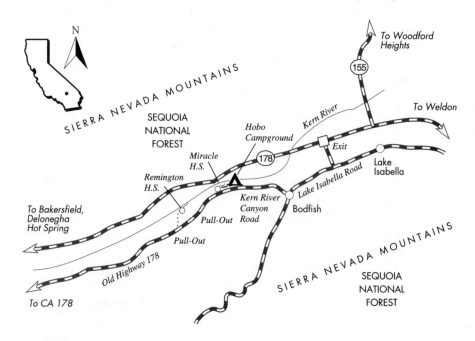

Miracle Hot Spring, California.

Access: Any vehicle can make the trip.
Water temperature: About 120 degrees F. at the hottest pool, varying depending upon the spring chosen. Most pools average 100 degrees F.
Nearby attractions: Lake Isabella, Kern River Canyon.
Services: None; gas, food, and lodging can be found 6 miles away at Lake Isabella.
Camping: Camping is permitted at adjacent Hobo Campground, managed by the Forest Service.
Map: USGS Lake Isabella, CA quadrangle (1:100,000 scale).
Finding the hot spring: From Bakersfield, travel east on California Highway 178 toward Lake Isabella. The highway will enter the Kern River Canyon. Travel upcanyon past the pullouts for Pyramid and Delonegha hot springs (Springs 74 and 76). From the Delonegha Hot Spring pullout, continue east for about 10.3 miles to the exit for Lake Isabella and Bodfish. Exit here and turn right, traveling away from the highway. The road will dead-end at Lake Isabella Road, where you turn right. Go east on Lake Isabella Rd. for about 1.4 miles to Kern River Canyon Road, where you turn right (north). Take this road (old CA 178) about 3.6 miles to Hobo Campground. Turn right into the campground and drive to the west end. There is a small parking area here. From the parking area, follow a small trail for 100 yards to several hot spring pools at the river's edge.

The hot spring: Another one-time hot spring resort, Miracle Hot Spring still offers a great soak. Hot spring water emerges from the side of the hill and is trapped in several pools of varying size and temperature. The hottest pool is too small to bathe in, and about 120 degrees F. The largest of the pools constructed with concrete and rock is about 105 degrees F. Although they are adjacent to the Kern River, these pools do not generally get inundated.

This is a beautiful setting and a great place for a bath. Because it is so close to a campground, however, the spring is well known, so your chances for privacy here are virtually nil. Common tradition is to wear bathing suits.

75

Delonegha Hot Spring

General description: A collection of hot springs on the edge of the Kern River. Three of the springs are located on private property and are off-limits, while a fourth is on public land and is accessible by river only.

Location: Central California, 10 miles west of Lake Isabella.

Primitive/developed: Primitive. Several concrete tubs were in place in the past, although they have been recently removed.

Best time of year: Late spring and summer. The river is too high at other times to make visiting the springs safe.

Restrictions: Although three of the springs are closed to public use, a fourth can be reached by raft from the river.

Access: A raft is required in order to avoid trespassing on private property.

Water temperature: About 120 degrees F. at the source, decreasing as it flows to the river.

Nearby attractions: Lake Isabella, Kern River Canyon.

Services: None; gas, food, and lodging can be found 10 miles away in Lake Isabella.

Camping: Camping is not permitted at the hot springs themselves. There are several Forest Service campgrounds in the immediate vicinity, including the Hobo campground.

Map: USGS Lake Isabella, CA quadrangle (1:100,000 scale).

Finding the hot spring: Your best bet on finding the springs is inquiring from one of the local rafting companies servicing the river. The springs can be reached from the road, but the only way to access the spring this way requires trespassing, which of course, I do not recommend. The hot springs are located approximately 1 mile upstream from a pullout, which is 26.4

Delonegha Hot Spring

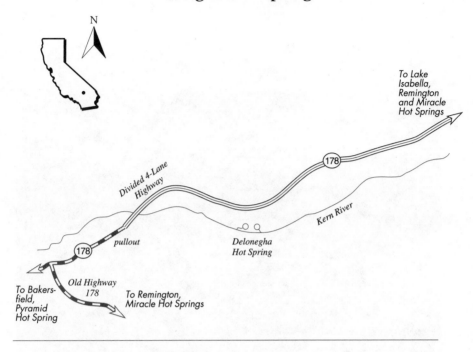

miles upstream from the beginning of the Kern River Canyon (or 22.2 miles from the pullout for Pyramid Hot Springs.)

The hot spring: Until recently, all four hot springs were open to public use. The owner of the three hot springs, Mr. Wan Mou Youn, previously offered access to the springs for a fee. Several large concrete and rock pools existed along the river side, making for wonderful soaking opportunities. Wan Mou Youn and his family hoped to develop a resort at the hot springs, and planned to build a bridge across the river for better access. They ran into trouble, however, from vandals, trespassers, and a lack of funding. As a result, the soaking pools were destroyed, and access to privately-owned springs was restricted. The fourth hot spring, lying closest to the river, is still accessible to the public. In order to reach the spring without trespassing, you must travel by boat. The spring has been frequented by locals for years, many of whom continue to visit, and in the process, trespass. I recommend that you visit this spring only when rafting the river.

Delonegha Hot Spring, California, in its former state. Visitors once enjoyed these soaking tubs, but because of vandalism and trespassing, the tubs were recently destroyed. Just one spring remains open to the public; it is accessible by river only.

76

Pyramid Hot Spring

General description: An obscure hot spring in the Kern River Canyon near Lake Isabella.

Location: Central California, about 20 miles east of Lake Isabella.

Primitive/developed: Primitive.

Best time of year: Year-round. Summers can be hot, and the pool may be submerged during extraordinarily high runoff.

Restrictions: None.

Access: Any vehicle can make the trip. The hot spring is accessible only in the summer months when the river is low. Do not attempt to cross the river when it is high. Exercise extreme caution.

Water temperature: About 105 degrees F. throughout the natural pool.

Nearby attractions: Lake Isabella, Kern River Canyon.

Services: None; gas, food, and lodging can be found 20 miles east in the town of Lake Isabella, or in Bakersfield, 15 miles west.

Camping: Camping is not permitted at the turnout in the road, but you wouldn't want to camp there. There is a Forest Service campground (Live Oak) 1 mile east.

Pyramid Hot Spring

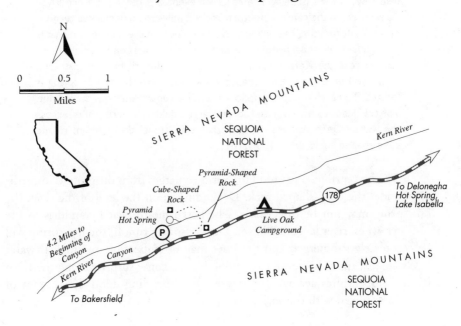

Pyramid Hot Spring, California.

Map: Sequoia National Forest map.
Finding the spring: Travel east on California Highway 178 from Bakersfield toward Lake Isabella. The road will eventually reach the Kern River Canyon. From the canyon mouth, travel 4.2 miles to an unmarked turnout on your left (north). The pullout has an iron pole in the middle of it that is about 5 feet tall, and a pyramid-shaped rock on the east end. Pull out here. Look across the Kern River from the pullout and slightly downstream. There will be a large, cube-shaped rock, under which the hot spring is located. To reach the spring, follow a faint trail upstream from the pullout. The trail leads to the river and several large boulders where you can cross the water. Once you are on the other side, travel downstream to the cube-shaped rock, about 100 yards.

The hot springs: Pyramid Hot Spring emerges from the ground immediately under the cube-shaped rock. Depending upon the level of the river, the hot spring may not be discernible. The best time to visit Pyramid is in the summer, when river levels are lower. During spring runoff, the hot spring will be completely submerged and the river may be impossible to cross. If water levels are just right, however, this spring is a welcome surprise along the Kern River. Temperatures average 105 degrees F., depending upon the amount of river water mixed with the spring water.

Although the spring is difficult to find, it is within view of the highway, and therefore does not offer the highest degree of privacy. Because it is so close to the highway, the spring can be reached rather quickly and makes an enjoyable diversion when passing through or visiting other springs in the region.

Be careful when crossing the river, and do not attempt to cross when water levels are high. Hundreds of people have lost their lives in the fast current of the Kern River in the past decades. Do not try to swim across, but instead stick to the boulders upstream, using care when stepping across. Contact Sequoia National Forest at (209) 784-1500, for further information.

MOJAVE DESERT

One of the largest deserts in the United States, the Mojave may seem empty and featureless to travelers who cross it on Interstate 15. Those who take the time to get off the main road and explore the region see much more. A wide variety of plant and animal life lives in the harsh climate of the Mojave, with its hot summers, bitterly cold winters, and exceedingly high winds. For years the Mojave was an area in which travelers simply wanted to get through on their way to settlements on the coast or points east. Later, however, the region's mineral wealth was discovered, and miners streamed in from all directions. More recently the U.S. military has recognized the usefulness of the desert for its various training missions. Today huge tracts of the desert are owned and operated by the military, in the form of bases such as China Lake Naval Weapons Center, Fort Irwin Military Reservation, and Edwards Air Force Base and Flight Test Center. Outdoor enthusiasts have also recognized the recreation opportunities provided by the largely unpopulated and undeveloped desert. In 1994, more than 1.4 million acres of the desert were set aside by the U.S. government as the Mojave National Preserve, protecting the archaeological, historical, and natural resources in the area.

77

Deep Creek

General description: A cluster of natural hot springs in an isolated canyon in the high desert. Deep Creek has become a favorite spot for those who like to go without clothing. Requires a gradual 6-mile hike or a steeper 2-mile one.
Location: Southern California, about 16 miles east of Hesperia.
Primitive/developed: Primitive.
Best time of year: Fall, winter, or spring. Summer can be hot. Avoid the shorter trail during high water levels (in early spring mostly) since the trail fords the river.
Restrictions: None at the spring itself. To take the shorter trail you must park at a private ranch, which allows parking for a fee.
Access: Most vehicles will have no problem with the graded dirt roads to either trailhead. Getting to the spring itself requires a hike of 6 miles one-way along a gentle trail or 2 miles one-way along an extremely steep trail.
Water temperature: About 110 degrees F. at the various sources, vary-

Deep Creek

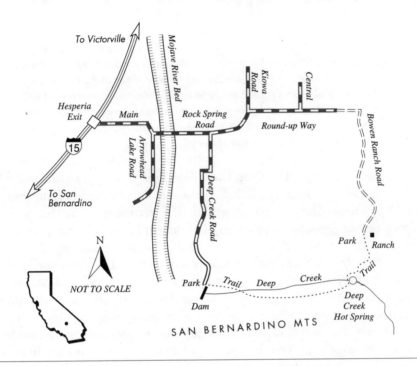

To Victorville

Mojave River Bed

Kiowa Road

Central

Hesperia Exit

Main

Rock Spring Road

Round-up Way

Bowen Ranch Road

15

Arrowhead Lake Road

To San Bernardino

Deep Creek Road

N

NOT TO SCALE

Park   Ranch

Park   Trail   Deep   Creek   Trail

Dam

Deep Creek Hot Spring

SAN BERNARDINO MTS

ing in the pools depending upon the amount of creek water admitted.

Nearby attractions: Lake Arrowhead, Big Bear City, Big Bear Lake.

Services: None; gas, food, and lodging can be found 16 miles away in the town of Hesperia.

Camping: Camping is not permitted in the canyon, at the springs, or at the parking area for the longer trail. You can pay a fee at the Bowen Ranch to camp at the parking area there, however. There also are campgrounds in the nearby San Bernardino Mountains at Silverwood Lake and Lake Arrowhead. Take Interstate 15 west to California Highway 138 east to reach San Bernardino National Forest.

Map: USGS Lake Arrowhead, CA quadrangle (7.5-minute scale).

Finding the springs: From Interstate 15 take the Hesperia exit and turn east onto Main Street. Follow Main Street for about 8 miles to a Y and Rock Springs Road. Go right on Rock Springs Rd. for about 1.8 miles to Deep Creek Road, and turn right. Follow Deep Creek Rd. until it turns to dirt. Then look for the dam and head for the southeast side of it. Park where you can and walk to the top of the dam along its paved service road. The trailhead for the 6-mile hike is to the left when facing the inside portion of the dam. A small metal sign on the side of the hill marks where the trailhead begins. The trail goes uphill steeply for the first few hundred yards, then levels out. Follow the trail for 6 miles, crossing the creek on a bridge after 2 miles. The trail will lead right to the spring.

To take the steeper, 2-mile trail take Rock Spring Road at the Y and go left. Follow Rock Spring Rd. about 2.8 miles to Roundup Way, then turn right. Take Roundup Rd. about 4.2 miles to Bowen Ranch Road, and turn right again. Follow this graded dirt road for 5.5 miles to the ranch itself and the parking area. Someone is often there to collect a parking fee and direct you to the trailhead. This trail is quite steep and slippery, not recommended if you are in poor shape or don't have good balance.

The hot springs: The Deep Creek Hot Springs are quite a find and will amaze you once you get there. Completely natural and undeveloped, the springs have become popular for obvious reasons. The water is generally clear and an almost perfect temperature (averaging 105 degrees F.), with several pools from which to choose. As with so many hot springs in this book, Deep Creek was once relatively unknown, but has become heavily visited. Visitors have done a good job of keeping this area pristine, however, free from trash and vandalism. As noted, many of the more recent (and more numerous) visitors to the spring prefer to go without clothing, in and out of the pools.

Remember that mileages to the springs are one-way only. Do not attempt to visit these springs if you don't think you can walk the round-trip in a day. Also bring plenty of water and food, and let someone know where you are going and when you expect to be back.

The San Bernardino Mountains offer high elevation relief in the desert summer. Several lakes are found there. The region is largely controlled by San Bernardino National Forest, but there are several small towns in the area with an abundance of year-round activities. To reach Lake Arrowhead, travel east on CA 138 off I-15 into the mountains for about 10 miles. To reach ski and resort areas at Big Bear City and Big Bear Lake, continue on California Highway 18 to Running Springs and travel east about 20 miles.

78

Tecopa Hot Springs

General description: A group of rustic hot spring resorts, a county-owned public pool, and a natural pond in the low desert of eastern California near Death Valley.

Location: Southeastern California, about 58 miles north of Baker.

Primitive/developed: The resorts and county pool are developed; the pond is primitive.

Best time of year: Fall, winter, or spring. Summer is too hot.

Restrictions: The resorts are private and require that you either be an overnight guest or pay a fee for day use. The county pool is always open, with no charge. There are no restrictions at the natural pond.

Access: Any vehicle can access the resorts and county pool, immediately off the paved highway. Most sturdy vehicles should have no problems getting to the pond, although the road may be impassable in extremely wet weather.

Water temperature: Varies depending upon venue.

Nearby attractions: Death Valley National Park, East Mojave Scenic Area.

Services: All services can be found in the small town of Tecopa.

Camping: There is a public campground on the outskirts of Tecopa, and camping is permitted at the pond, although there are no developed sites there.

Map: California State Highway map.

Finding the spring: From Baker and Interstate 15, travel north on California Highway 127 for about 52 miles to the turnoff for Tecopa. Turn right (east) and drive another 5 miles to town, where there are several resorts to choose from. The county-run pool and bathhouse are on your right as you enter town. To get to the natural pond, take the first road north of the county pool to the right (at the "slow" sign). Drive on this road for approximately 0.3 mile past a pond on your left. Go beyond this pond on the lesser developed of two roads, following it another 0.6 mile as it becomes less and less of a road. Head for a palm tree and other green foliage where the small pond is located.

The hot springs: This rather run-down town is hot spring heaven if you aren't looking for fancy resorts. Most of the hotels are older and have seen better days, and many are now closed. The resorts all have hot pools for use of their guests and in some cases for day use. Baths range from common warm pools to individual private tubs.

Some of the resorts that were still open at the time of publication:

Ali Baba's Hide-A-Way   (619) 852-4438
Delight's Hot Spa   (619) 852-4343
Tecopa Hot Springs   619) 852-4373

The county pool and bathhouse require nude bathing only, with separate facilities for men and women. There is no charge at this facility, and the pool is quite invigorating.

The natural hot pond is at the end of a rather faint road east of town. The pond is about 5 feet by 5 feet, and 3 feet deep, at 100 degrees F. The pond is not well known, so you should be able to find a time to have it to yourself. The area around the pond is not altogether scenic, though, since many careless people have left trash and other debris. If you can block the junk out of your mind, the surrounding desert views are beautiful.

Tecopa Consolidated Mining Company: Tecopa is one of many small desert communities owing their existence to mining. Silver-lead ores were dis-

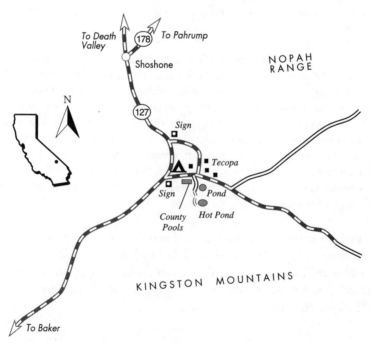

Tecopa Hot Springs

covered in the area in 1865 and mined until 1882. The mine apparently contained enough ore to warrant the construction of a ten-stamp mill and three furnaces, plus the digging of a tunnel more than a thousand feet into the mountain.

By the turn of the last century, as copper became a valued commodity, miners increasingly sought out sources of the metal. With the increased mining activity at Goldfield and Tonopah in the early 1900s, miners fanned out in the surrounding countryside. In 1904 copper was discovered southwest of Death Valley Junction, and the townsite established nearby was named Greenwater. By 1907, more than 700 people lived in the town, and a telephone line connected it to the mining community of Rhyolite to the northwest. Rampant speculation followed the miners, with more than thirty companies forming to take advantage of Greenwater's anticipated riches. By summer 1907, the town included a telegraph, two newspapers, a bank, a boardinghouse, several stores, and many more saloons. But the ore body quickly petered out, and the town was all but deserted by September of the same year.

To take advantage of the heralded wealth of the Greenwater mines, the Tonopah & Tidewater Railroad began extending its line toward Greenwater. When Greenwater's collapse came, however, the line had only made it to the Amargosa River. The line did reach the vicinity of Tecopa, giving the Noonday and Gunsite mines an outlet for their silver. The Tecopa Consolidated Mining Company built a railroad from the mines to the Tecopa station for the Tonopah & Tidewater, transporting ore to smelters in Utah. The mines continued to operate from 1912 through 1928, producing more than $3,000,000 worth of silver and lead.

Santa Barbara Region

Long a haven for artists and movie stars, Santa Barbara mixes the spectacular scenery of the Pacific Coast with city amenities and charm in an understandably sought-after location. Several beaches line the Santa Barbara coast from the University of California at Santa Barbara in the north to Carpinteria in the south. Depending upon what you want, there is bound to be a beach to your liking. Downtown, State Street offers a plethora of shopping, dining, and nightlife opportunities.

The towering Santa Ynez Mountains offer a splendid backdrop for the city. The mountains also offer countless getaway opportunities for those tired of the crowded coast. Although the mountains are rugged and largely unpopulated, there are several roads leading up into them. Deep in Los Padres National Forest, many of these roads are dirt and minimally maintained. Campgrounds, picnic spots, hiking routes, and biking trails provide outdoor recreation for the mountainous region.

Although the area is rather dry, there are a few year-round waterways in the mountains. Big and Little Caliente hot springs are located in this rugged terrain and can be reached by a few hours' drive. U.S. Highway 101 connects Santa Barbara with other communities to the north and south, passing Gaviota State Park within which Las Cruces Hot Spring is located. Only 26 miles from Santa Barbara, this hot spring is easily visited in a half-day.

79

Big Caliente Hot Spring

(See map on page 212.)

General description: A natural hot spring piped into a cement pool in the rugged mountains above Santa Barbara. Well-known, Big Caliente experiences heavy visitation on weekends.
Location: Southern California, about 26 miles north of Santa Barbara.
Primitive/developed: The spring has been developed, with changing rooms and a bathroom but an otherwise primitive setting.
Best time of year: Spring or fall. Summer can be hot, and the road can be difficult or impassable in wet weather.
Restrictions: The pool is in a national forest, so all Forest Service rules must be obeyed. Bathing suits are customary.

Big Caliente Hot Spring.

Access: A high-clearance vehicle is best, although many passenger cars make the trip. Do not attempt the road in wet weather.

Water temperature: About 110 degrees F. at the source. The pool itself stays at about 105 degrees F., but can be lowered by diverting the source.

Nearby attractions: Pacific Coast, Santa Barbara, Little Caliente Hot Spring.

Services: None, but all services can be found 26 miles away in Santa Barbara.

Camping: Camping is not permitted, but there are several developed Forest Service campgrounds on the road to the spring and on the road to Little Caliente Hot Spring. Contact Los Padres National Forest for further information.

Map: USGS Cuyama, CA quadrangle (1:100,000 scale).

Finding the spring: From Santa Barbara, travel north on U.S. Highway 101, taking the Milpas exit (California Highway 144). Follow the signs for CA 144 through Santa Barbara, turning right on Mason, then left on Salinas, and right at a four-way traffic circle. After about 6 miles CA 144 will intersect with California Highway 192 (Stanwood Drive). Turn left and follow Stanwood for 1.2 miles to El Cielito, then turn right. Be sure to stay on El Cielito for 0.5 mile to Gibraltar Road, where you turn right again. Follow Gibraltar Road for another 6.5 miles to East Camino Cielo, where there is a Forest Service sign. Turn right here. This is Forest Road 5N12, paved and windy for the first 6.8 miles. The road turns to dirt and winds the rest of the way to the spring. Follow FR 5N12 and all signs to Big Caliente, staying left 1 mile after the road turns to dirt. About 5 miles after the road turns to dirt you will arrive at Juncal Campground, where you will turn left on Forest Road 5N15, marked by signs for Big Caliente. Continue another 3 miles to Forest Road 5N16, where you turn right. Follow this road another 2.5 miles to where the road dead-ends at the parking lot for the hot spring. The spring will be on your right as you enter the parking lot.

The drive to the spring from Santa Barbara is long and slow. Allow several hours to get there and several to get back. Do not rush, since in many places the road is slippery and there are large dropoffs on one side.

The hot springs: Despite its rather rugged location, Big Caliente has had many improvements made to it. The hot spring source is piped into a rather elaborate concrete tub built into the ground. The hot springs are also equipped with a concrete dressing room and latrines. The concrete tub is about 7 feet by

Big Caliente Hot Spring, Little Caliente Hot Spring

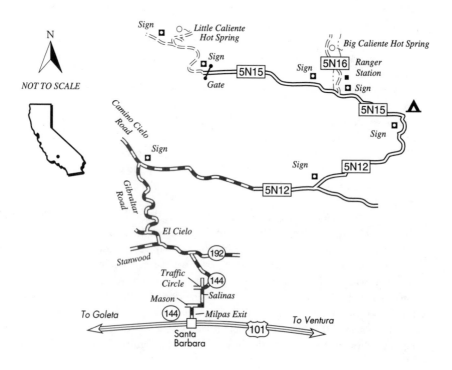

4 feet and 3 feet deep, ideal for several people to bathe in at once. The water is rather hot, so you may want to divert the source water out of the pond for a while before bathing. A light trickle of water sprays over the spring from the source, creating a mild shower effect.

This hot spring is relatively well-known, and heavily visited on weekends. Bathing suits are universally worn. During the week you may be fortunate enough to have the spring to yourself. There are other smaller sources of hot spring water upstream from the main pool at Big Caliente. These other sources are primarily located below a trailhead at the far end of the parking area. The smaller springs have a low flow rate, and require digging to make a workable soaking experience.

80

Little Caliente Hot Spring

(See map on page 212.)

General description: A less developed hot spring than Big Caliente, Little Caliente is farther out and may require a 2-mile hike or bike ride from the closest parking area if a gate is closed. Little Caliente Hot Spring sees many visitors on weekends, but is less busy during the week.

Location: Southern California, about 29 miles north of Santa Barbara.

Primitive/developed: Primitive, except for construction of a crude cement pool.

Best time of year: Spring or fall. Summer can be hot, and the road can be difficult to impassable in wet weather.

Restrictions: The hot spring is in the national forest, so all Forest Service rules apply.

Access: A high-clearance vehicle is best, although many passenger cars make the trip. Do not attempt the road in wet weather. The last 0.5 mile is rather rough. If the gate at Mono Hill is closed, you will have to hike or bike 2 more miles to the spring.

Water temperature: About 110 degrees F. at the source, 105 degrees F. in the upper tub, and 103 degrees F. in the lower tub.

Nearby attractions: Pacific Coast, Santa Barbara, Big Caliente Hot Spring.

Services: None, but all service can be found 29 miles away in Santa Barbara.

Camping: Camping is not permitted at the spring, but there are several developed Forest Service campgrounds on the road in. Contact Los Padres National Forest for further information and regulations.

Map: USGS Cuyama, CA quadrangle (1:100,000 scale).

Little Caliente Hot Spring.

Finding the spring: South of Santa Barbara, travel north on U.S. Highway 101, taking the Milpas exit (California Highway 144). Follow signs for CA 144 through Santa Barbara, turning right on Mason, then left on Salinas, then right at a four-way traffic circle. After about 6 miles CA 144 intersects California Highway 192 (Stanwood Drive). Turn left and follow Stanwood for 1.2 miles to El Cielito, then turn right. Be sure to stay on El Cielito for 0.5 mile to Gibraltar Road, where you turn right. Follow Gibraltar Rd. for another 6.5 miles to East Camino Cielo, where there is a Forest Service sign. Turn right here. This is Forest Road 5N12, paved and windy for the first 6.8 miles. The road turns to dirt and winds the rest of the way to the spring.

Follow 5N12 and all signs to Big Caliente, staying left 1 mile after the road turns to dirt. About 5 miles after the road turns to dirt you will arrive at Juncal Campground, where you will turn left on Forest Road 5N15. Continue another 3 miles to Forest Road 5N16, which goes to Big Caliente. Stay straight here, following the sign to Little Caliente. Continue on FR 5N15 for about 3.5 miles, crossing a creek and reaching a gate at Mono Hill. If the gate is closed, park here and walk or bike the last 2 miles to the spring. From Mono Hill after another mile you will reach Mono Campground, where you may want to park your car if it does not have high clearance. Stay on the main road uphill to another sign for Little Caliente

Spring, where you will turn right. Follow this road (in poor condition) for 1 more mile to the spring. After a mile the road will climb up a hill, and the spring will be to your right, emerging from a canyon with a little bit of greenery. Look for wooden steps and a metal post sticking out of the ground.

As with the drive to Big Caliente, allow several hours each way since the dirt road is curvy and slippery. Take it slow through the many blind curves, being careful near steep dropoffs.

The hot spring: Little Caliente is a pleasant place to visit in fall and spring, when the weather is not too hot. The source is a small trickle of water that is piped into two separate concrete tubs. Both tubs are rather primitive, and don't detract from the wilderness experience. Both tubs provide nice soaking opportunities. This hot spring is visited often in summer, so you should not expect privacy. During the week, however, you will find few people and may have it to yourself.

81

Gaviota State Park (Las Cruces) Hot Spring

General description: A natural, murky hot spring in a pleasant canyon with substantial vegetation, less than a mile off U.S. Highway 101. A 0.75-mile trail takes you to the spring.

Location: Southern California, about 20 miles east of the town of Lompoc.

Primitive/developed: Primitive.

Best time of year: Year-round. Summer can be hot, but vegetation at the spring provides sufficient shade to keep you cool.

Restrictions: The hot spring is on state park land, and all park rules apply. The hot spring is open to day use only, and there is a fee for parking.

Access: Any vehicle can make the trip to the parking area only a short distance off a major highway. A 0.75-mile hike is required to reach the spring.

Water temperature: About 100 degrees F. at the source, and 90 degrees F. in the small pond where the best bathing is. A larger pond with a waterfall is about 80 degrees F.

Nearby attractions: Gaviota State Beach, Buellton.

Services: None, but gas, food, and lodging can be found 20 miles away in Lompoc or 31 miles away in Santa Barbara.

Camping: Camping is not permitted at the spring or the parking area. There are several state campgrounds to the south along the beach.

Gaviota State Park (Las Cruces) Hot Spring

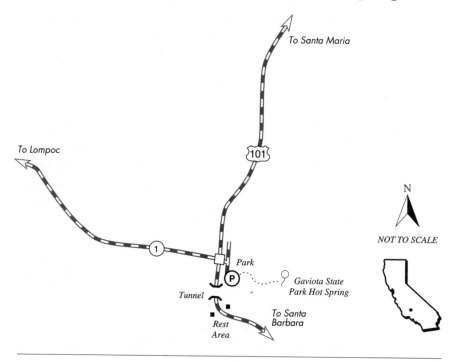

Map: California State Highway map.
Finding the spring: From Santa Barbara travel north on U.S. Highway 101 to the exit for California Highway 1 toward Lompoc. Exit here, staying on the east side of the highway, and turn right on a frontage road paralleling the highway to the south. This road will lead you to the parking area for Gaviota State Park. Park here and pick up the 0.75-mile trail to the spring. The trailhead is well-marked.

The hot springs: Despite its murky appearance, this hot spring provides a great soak. Surrounding vegetation makes you feel like you're in a jungle and keeps the location cool. The main pool is fed by a small natural hot spring, which maintains a temperature of about 100 degrees F. The water overflows from this smaller pool as a waterfall into a larger pool, which is about 80 degrees F. This lower pool is less appealing, due to moss and algae growth plus large amounts of leaves and other vegetation falling into it. So far the hot spring has been kept clean and free of trash, thanks no doubt in large part to hard-working park rangers. The spring is only open during daylight hours, since the parking lot closes at dusk.

Highline Hot Well.

SAN DIEGO AND IMPERIAL COUNTIES

The low desert Imperial Valley is now an agricultural center, made possible by irrigation through canals drawing water from the Colorado River. The largest feature in the region is the Salton Sea, a lake with no outlet and polluted by agricultural runoff and sewage. Anza–Borrego Desert State Park lies west of the Imperial Valley, a desert environment punctuated by mountain ranges and low hills. The Anza–Borrego region is a desert lover's paradise. Several different desert biotas intersect in the park. Camping, hiking, biking, and off-highway driving are some of the region's more popular activities.

The main means of access to the region is along Interstate 8, which runs due east from San Diego and south of Anza–Borrego across the Imperial Valley and, eventually, into Arizona. Highline Hot Well lies only a few yards from the interstate. Agua Caliente lies in the southern part of the state park, along County Road S-2.

Avoid this region during summer months, when daytime air temperatures exceed 110 degrees F. with regularity. Winter is the best time to visit both Agua Caliente and Highline Hot Well, since lower temperatures make the soaking more enjoyable.

82

Highline Hot Well

General description: A large hot well piped into a rather elaborate concrete pool immediately off Interstate 8.

Location: Southern California, about 15 miles east of El Centro.

Primitive/developed: The hot well itself is developed, but the surrounding area is undeveloped save for restrooms.

Best time of year: Fall, winter, or spring. Summer is far too hot, with daytime temperatures often exceeding 120 degrees F.

Restrictions: Daytime use only. The well is on state land, and camping is not allowed at the pool itself.

Access: Any vehicle can make the trip, since the hot spring is immediately off an interstate highway.

Water temperature: About 120 degrees F. at the source, cooling to about 105 degrees F. in the pool.

Nearby attractions: Salton Sea, Colorado River.

Services: None, but all services can be found about 15 miles away in El Centro.

Camping: Camping is not permitted at the pool itself, but there is a large

---

Highline Hot Well

campground across the road where there are many undeveloped spaces.

Maps: California State Highway Map, Imperial County map.

Finding the spring: From El Centro travel east on Interstate 8 for about 15 miles to the Van der Plas exit. Exit and cross over the freeway. Turn right as you pass over the freeway onto the frontage road (Evan Hughes Highway). Take the frontage road for about 1 mile to a campground on your left and a parking area on your right. Park here. The hot well is immediately downhill from the restrooms, against the interstate.

The hot springs: Highline Hot Well is not the place you want to go if you want nature and seclusion. The pool is immediately off a major interstate highway, across the road from a popular campground, and has no views of the surrounding countryside. Despite this, the pool itself is excellent for a hot bath. Water from the well that supplies the pool is about 120 degrees F. and cools to an almost perfect 105 degrees F. for an invigorating soak. There is also a mild shower effect as water sprays over the pool. The pool is large and deeper than most (4 feet), about 6 feet by 6 feet in dimension. There is also a smaller pool adjacent to the main one, slightly cooler and not quite as inviting. The pool is well maintained by campers who tend to stay at this location for weeks at a time during the winter.

83

Agua Caliente Hot Spring

General description: A county-run park with a large indoor warm pool and an outdoor pool fed by a natural hot spring in the low desert.

Location: Southern California, within Anza-Borrego Desert State Park, about 95 miles from San Diego.

Primitive/developed: Developed.

Best time of year: The park is only open from September to May.

Restrictions: This is a county park and campground. The pools are open to campers and to day users for a fee.

Access: Any vehicle can make the trip, since the hot spring is immediately off a paved highway.

Water temperature: About 95 degrees F. in the indoor pool, and 90 degrees F. in the outside pool.

Nearby attractions: Anza–Borrego Desert State Park.

Services: None; the closest gasoline, food, and supplies can be found about 35 miles away in the small town of Ocotillo.

Camping: Developed campsites are available for $10 per night for tents, $14 for full RV hook-ups, and $12 for partial hook-ups.

Agua Caliente Hot Spring

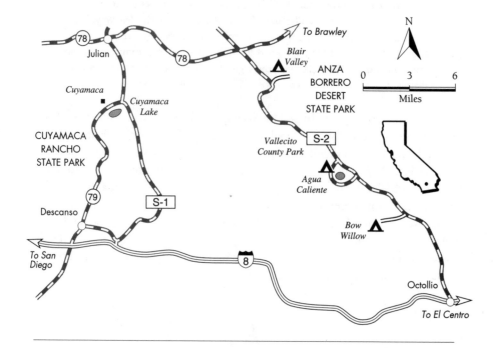

Maps: California State Highway Map, Anza–Borrego Desert State Park Map.

Finding the spring: From San Diego travel east on Interstate 8 to the exit for Ocotillo Wells and County Road S-2. Travel north on CR S-2 for about 35 miles to Agua Caliente County Park, where you will turn left to reach the park's entry kiosk. Pay fees here and drive to the back of the campground where the pools are located.

The hot springs: The large indoor warm pool is a great place for a communal soak when the weather is cool. The pool is equipped with Jacuzzi-like jets and hovers around 95 degrees F. The park is equipped with showers, restrooms, and dressing rooms. This indoor pool is reserved for adults only, though kids are free to use the outdoor pool (with proper supervision), which is a little cooler (90 degrees F.). Both pools are well cared for and kept clean. The park is owned by the County of San Diego, but is within the larger Anza–Borrego Desert State Park, one of the most beautiful desert parks, with thousands of acres of fascinating country. The state park can be reached at (619) 767-4684. Agua Caliente County Park can be reached at (619) 565-3600.

FURTHER READING

Garside, Larry J. and John H. Schilling. *Thermal Waters of Nevada*. Bulletin 91, Nevada Bureau of Mines and Geology. Reno, Nev.: Mackay School of Mines, University of Nevada, Reno, 1979.

Lund, John W. Balneological use of thermal and mineral waters in the U.S.A. *Geothermics*. 25:103-147, 1996.

Wheeler, Sessions. *The Desert Lake: The Story of Nevada's Pyramid Lake*. Caldwell, Idaho: Caxton Printers, Ltd., 1980.

Wheeler, Sessions. *The Nevada Desert*. Caldwell, Idaho: Caxton Printers, Ltd., 1982.

Vredenburgh, Larry M., Gary L. Shumway, and Russell Hartill. *Desert Fever: An Overview of Mining in the California Desert*. Canoga Park, Calif.: Living West Press, 1981.

FOR MORE INFORMATION

Bureau of Land Management

California State Office
2800 Cottage Way, E-2841
Sacramento, CA 95825
(916) 978-4754

Nevada State Office
850 Harvard Way
P.O. Box 12000
Reno, NV 89520
(702) 785-6501

Fallon, NV Office
(702) 885-6000

Hidden Cave
(702) 423-3677

USDA Forest Service

Humboldt National Forest
2035 Last Chance Rd.
Elko, NV 89801
(702) 738-5171

Inyo National Forest
Lee Vining Ranger District
P.O. Box 429
Lee Vining, CA 93541
(619) 647-3000

Mono Lake Visitor Center
(619) 647-3000

Los Padres National Forest
6144 Calle Real
Goleta, CA 93117
(805) 683-6711

Big Sur Ranger Station
(408) 667-2423

Mendocino National Forest
420 E. Laurel St.
Willows, CA 95988
(916) 934-2350

Upper Lake Ranger Station
(707) 275-2361

Modoc National Forest
800 West 12th St.
Alturas, CA 96101
(916) 233-5811

San Bernardino National Forest
1824 S. Commercecenter Circle
San Bernadino, CA 92408-3430
(909) 383-5588

Sequoia National Forest
900 West Grand Ave.
Porterville, CA 93257-2035
(209) 784-1500

Lake Isabella
(619) 379-5646

Toiyabe National Forest
1200 Franklin Way
Sparks, NV 89431
(702) 331-6444

Private Hot Springs

Ali Baba's (Hide-A-Way)
Box 101
Tecopa, CA 92389
(619) 852-4438

Bailey's Hot Springs
P.O. Box 387
Beatty, CA 89003
(702) 553-2395

Big Bend Hot Springs
P.O. Box 81
Big Bend, CA 96011
(916) 337-6680

Carson River Hot Springs
1500 Hot Springs Rd.
Carson City, NV 89701
(702) 882-9863

Delight's Hot Spa
Box 368
Tecopa, CA 92389
(619) 852-4343

Drakesbad Guest Ranch
2150 Main St. #5
Red Bluff, CA 96080
(916) 529-1512

Esalen Institute
Big Sur, CA
(408) 667-3047

Gerlach Hot Springs
(702) 557-0220

Sierra Hot Springs
P.O. Box 366
Sierraville, CA 96126
(916) 994-3773

Steamboat Hot Springs
(702) 853-0858

Tassajara Springs
Carmel Valley, CA
(415) 431-3771

Tecopa Hot Springs
Box 420
Tecopa, CA 92389
(619) 852-4373

Vichy Springs
2605 Vichy Springs Rd.
Ukiah, CA 95842
(707) 462-9515

Walleys Hot Spring Resort
2001 Foothill Rd.
Genoa, NV 89411
(702) 782-8155

California State Parks

Grover Hot Springs State Park
Box 188
Markleeville, CA 96120
(916) 694-2248

Bodie State Historic Park
P.O. Box 515
Bridgeport, CA 93517
(619) 647-6445

Anza–Borrego Desert State Park
Palm Canyon Drive
Borrego Springs, CA 92004
(619) 767-4684

Nevada State Parks

Valley of Fire State Park
Nevada Highway 167
Overton, NV 89040
(702) 397-2088

**National Recreation Areas,
National Parks, and
National Monuments**

Death Valley National Park
P.O. Box 579
Death Valley, CA 92328
(619) 786-2331

Lake Mead
National Recreation Area
601 Nevada Highway
Boulder City, NV 89005
(702) 293-8907

Alan Bible Visitor Center
(702) 293-8906

Hoover Dam
(702) 293-8321

Lake Mead Cruises
(702) 293-6180

Lava Beds National Monument
(916) 667-2282

Lassen Volcanic National Park
Box 100
Mineral, CA 96063-0100
(916) 595-4444

San Diego County

Agua Caliente County Park
(619) 565-3600

Other Agencies

MISTIX (campground reservations):
1-800-444-PARK

Pyramid Lake Paiute Ranger Station:
(702) 476-0132

Pyramid Lake Paiute Tribe:
(702) 574-1002

Willow Beach Resort:
(520) 767-3311

ABOUT THE AUTHOR

A professional historian by trade, Matt Bischoff has always enjoyed the open spaces of the American West. Raised by a geologist, Matt grew up with a deeper understanding of the earth's processes. Hot springs have fascinated him since before he can remember and finding new ones is one of his favorite pastimes. Understanding the history surrounding each hot spring adds another layer of enjoyment, and he seeks out lost stories for each region he visits. He has explored California and Nevada extensively, and feels that the hot springs described in this book offer travelers some of the best country in the West.

After receiving his bachelor's degree in History and Geology at the University of California, Davis, Matt continued his study of the American frontier at the University of Nevada, Reno, where he received a master's degree in History and Historical Archaeology. Since that time he has worked for several private consulting firms in San Diego, at Edwards Air Force Base, and in Tucson, Arizona, where he currently resides.

Author preparing for trip in the Eastern Sierra.

FALCONGUIDES® Leading the Way

FIELD GUIDES
Bitterroot: Montana State Flower
Canyon Country Wildflowers
Central Rocky Mountains
    Wildflowers
Great Lakes Berry Book
New England Berry Book
Ozark Wildflowers
Pacific Northwest Berry Book
Plants of Arizona
Rare Plants of Colorado
Rocky Mountain Berry Book
Scats & Tracks of the Pacific
    Coast States
Scats & Tracks of the
    Rocky Mountains
Southern Rocky Mountain
    Wildflowers
Tallgrass Prairie Wildflowers
Western Trees
Wildflowers of Southwestern
    Utah
Willow Bark and Rosehips

FISHING GUIDES
Fishing Alaska
Fishing the Beartooths
Fishing Florida
Fishing Glacier National Park
Fishing Maine
Fishing Montana
Fishing Wyoming
Fishing Yellowstone
    National Park

ROCKHOUNDING GUIDES
Rockhounding Arizona
Rockhounding California
Rockhounding Colorado
Rockhounding Montana
Rockhounding Nevada
Rockhound's Guide to New
    Mexico
Rockhounding Texas
Rockhounding Utah
Rockhounding Wyoming

MORE GUIDEBOOKS
Backcountry Horseman's
    Guide to Washington
Camping California's
    National Forests
Exploring Canyonlands &
    Arches National Parks
Exploring Hawaii's Parklands
Exploring Mount Helena
Exploring Southern California
    Beaches
Recreation Guide to WA
    National Forests
Touring California & Nevada
    Hot Springs
Touring Colorado Hot Springs
Touring Montana & Wyoming
    Hot Springs
Trail Riding Western
    Montana
Wild Country Companion
Wilderness Directory
Wild Montana
Wild Utah

BIRDING GUIDES
Birding Minnesota
Birding Montana
Birding Northern California
Birding Texas
Birding Utah

PADDLING GUIDES
Floater's Guide to Colorado
Paddling Minnesota
Paddling Montana
Paddling Okefenokee
Paddling Oregon
Paddling Yellowstone & Grand
    Teton National Parks

HOW-TO GUIDES
Avalanche Aware
Backpacking Tips
Bear Aware
Desert Hiking Tips
Hiking with Dogs
Leave No Trace
Mountain Lion Alert
Reading Weather
Route Finding
Using GPS
Wilderness First Aid
Wilderness Survival

WALKING
Walking Colorado Springs
Walking Denver
Walking Portland
Walking St. Louis
Walking Virginia Beach

■ *To order any of these books, check with your local bookseller*
*or call FALCON® at **1-800-582-2665**.*
Visit us on the world wide web at:
www.FalconOutdoors.com

FALCON®

FALCON GUIDES® Leading the Way™

HIKING GUIDES

Best Hikes Along the Continental Divide
Hiking Alaska
Hiking Arizona
Hiking Arizona's Cactus Country
Hiking the Beartooths
Hiking Big Bend National Park
Hiking the Bob Marshall Country
Hiking California
Hiking California's Desert Parks
Hiking Carlsbad Caverns
   and Guadalupe Mtns. National Parks
Hiking Colorado
Hiking Colorado, Vol. II
Hiking Colorado's Summits
Hiking Colorado's Weminuche Wilderness
Hiking the Columbia River Gorge
Hiking Florida
Hiking Georgia
Hiking Glacier & Waterton Lakes National Parks
Hiking Grand Canyon National Park
Hiking Grand Staircase-Escalante/Glen Canyon
Hiking Grand Teton National Park
Hiking Great Basin National Park
Hiking Hot Springs in the Pacific Northwest
Hiking Idaho
Hiking Maine
Hiking Michigan
Hiking Minnesota
Hiking Montana
Hiking Mount Rainier National Park
Hiking Mount St. Helens
Hiking Nevada

Hiking New Hampshire
Hiking New Mexico
Hiking New York
Hiking the North Cascades
Hiking Northern Arizona
Hiking Olympic National Park
Hiking Oregon
Hiking Oregon's Eagle Cap Wilderness
Hiking Oregon's Mount Hood/Badger Creek
Hiking Oregon's Three Sisters Country
Hiking Pennsylvania
Hiking Shenandoah
Hiking the Sierra Nevada
Hiking South Carolina
Hiking South Dakota's Black Hills Country
Hiking Southern New England
Hiking Tennessee
Hiking Texas
Hiking Utah
Hiking Utah's Summits
Hiking Vermont
Hiking Virginia
Hiking Washington
Hiking Wisconsin
Hiking Wyoming
Hiking Wyoming's Cloud Peak Wilderness
Hiking Wyoming's Wind River Range
Hiking Yellowstone National Park
Hiking Zion & Bryce Canyon National Parks
Wild Montana
Wild Country Companion
Wild Utah

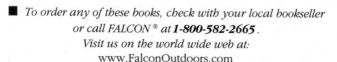

■ *To order any of these books, check with your local bookseller*
*or call FALCON® at **1-800-582-2665**.*
Visit us on the world wide web at:
www.FalconOutdoors.com